MW01122437

naked at school

THREE PLAYS FOR TEENS

naked at school

THREE PLAYS FOR TEENS

Chris Craddock

 Prairie Play Series: 21/Series Editor: Diane Bessai

Canadian Cataloguing in Publication Data
Craddock, Chris, 1972-
    Naked at school

    ISBN 1-896300-46-4

    1. Young adult drama, Canadian (English)* I. Title. PS8555.R238N34
2001   jC812'.54   C00-911520-X PR9199.3.C73N34 2001

Editor for the press: Anne Nothof
Cover photo: J. Alleyne Photography
Cover and interior design: Ruth Linka
Interior photos have been produced with the kind permission of the photographers.
Posters: Designed by Andy Laskiwsky, appearing courtesy of Azimuth Theatre.

Canadian   Patrimoine
Heritage   canadien

THE CANADA COUNCIL | LE CONSEIL DES ARTS
FOR THE ARTS | DU CANADA
SINCE 1957 | DEPUIS 1957

NeWest Press acknowledges the support of the Canada Council for the Arts and The Alberta Foundation for the Arts for our publishing program. We also acknowledge the financial support of the Government of Canada through the Book Publishing Industry Development Program (BPIDP) for our publishing activities.

NeWest Press
201-8540-109 Street
Edmonton, Alberta
T6G 1E6
T: (780) 432-9427
F: (780) 433-3179
www.newestpress.com

2   3   4   5   04   03

PRINTED AND BOUND IN CANADA

To Lesli, Dana, Kurt, Carley, Kalyn, Stacey and Derek.

Contents

Playography

Other Plays:

The Godling. First produced 1992, Those Terrible Children Theatre, Edmonton.

Biting Gently Then Licking. First produced 1992, Those Terrible Children Theatre, Edmonton.

SuperEd. First produced 1996, Those Terrible Children Theatre, Edmonton.

Indulgences. First produced 1996, F.I.N.E. Productions, Edmonton.

HA! (with Wes Borg). First produced 1998, Those Terrible Children Theatre, Edmonton.

Tranny Get Your Gun (with Darrin Hagen). First produced 1998, Guys in Disguise Theatre, Edmonton.

On Being a Peon. First produced 1999, Rapid Fire Theatre, Edmonton.

Men are Stoopid, Women are Cra-azy (with Darrin Hagen). First produced 1999, Guys in Disguise Theatre, Edmonton.

The Critic. First produced 2000, Rapid Fire Theatre, Edmonton.

Lil' Orphan Tranny (with Darrin Hagen). First produced 2000, Guys in Disguise Theatre, Edmonton.

Moving Along. First produced 2000, Theatre of the New Heart, Edmonton.

Monster Club (with Wes Borg). First produced 2001, Fringe Theatre Adventures, Edmonton.

Awards:

Elizabeth Sterling Haynes Award for:

Outstanding Achievement in Theatre for Young Audiences (Playwright) for *The Day Billy Lived*, 1996.

Outstanding Performance by an Actor in a Fringe Production for *HA!*, 1998.

Best Production of a Collective for *On Being a Peon*, 1999.

City of Edmonton Enbridge Award for Emerging Artist, 2000.

Introduction

When I was just out of school, acting school rather than writing school mind you, I saw an ad in *SEE Magazine*. It was calling for submissions of scripts on the topic of teen suicide. Since I fancied myself a bit of a writer and had taken twenty-two Tylenols in a bad moment at fourteen, I thought I was the man for the job. I had no idea what I was getting into. In the workshop of *The Day Billy Lived*, an earnest social worker leaned into my face and said, "You realize kids are going to attempt suicide after seeing this play." I became so frightened that I almost vomited right into her glasses. This was serious stuff, and me, I'm a showman, with only a vague sort of social conscience that was getting its first workout, right there in the rehearsal hall. I had thrown my hat into the ring of social action theatre and was now a social activist, and a professional one at that. I had to take a deep breath and accept a larger responsibility than I had realized I'd asked for, and what's more, I had to scramble right out that afternoon and get me some points of view. While I was out looking for them, I found I had them all along.

During the period between having *The Day Billy Lived* accepted for production and its first performance (almost two years), I did a bit of research into Theatre for Young Audiences. I found that many artists seem to have a dismissive attitude to it. Everyone seems to regard it as a sort of stepping stone, a fine paycheque if you needed it, but something less than art. I thought about why and here's what I came up with: Theatre for Young Audiences too often falls into a critical gap between kids who don't feel empowered to express an opinion and adults who don't expect to enjoy it in the first place. Consequently, artists can too easily misjudge the power of this theatre. These artists get the first chance at the audiences of the future, and this is no small responsibility. We must show them the best theatre we can; we must strive to speak to them directly, in their own language, to move them, to enrapture them. When they're adults and theatre already holds a special place in their consciousness, then we can risk boring them. At least they'll come back.

This was one of the points of view I had developed. And my good friend Sophie Lees, who helped me to form these plays and directed all of them, agrees with me. She is one of the most conscientious and hardworking artists I've had the pleasure to know. Way better than me, and that's a fact.

Now that I was a confirmed fighter of the good fight in Theatre for Young Audiences, I had to tackle how. You see, most TYA goes on in schools, and schools are more than educational institutions. They are political and social institutions, and very touchy ones at that. To speak to kids directly and in an unpedantic fashion, you have to be a bit sneaky. You have to strike a balance between what you know kids know and what parents and teachers are willing to admit kids know. You have to think back and remember yourself at that age. And you must try to avoid preaching . . . and foul language . . . and also blasphemy. Within these restrictions is a marvellous opportunity for subversion, and I believe kids watch out for subversion and love it to bits.

In my play about drugs and alcohol, *Wrecked*, I knew I wouldn't get far trying to convince kids that there was no fun at all in drinking and doing drugs at parties. I myself drank and did drugs at parties all the time when I was a teen, and had lots of great fun. But I also got into lots of scrapes while drinking and doing drugs, and there were many times that it was only dumb luck that I didn't end up dead or arrested or kicked out of school. I hope the play presents options and consequences to help teens make good choices, while still having fun at parties.

In my play about sex, *Do it Right*, I had an even touchier subject, loaded with political and religious landmines. Many people believe that sex education leads to sex. They are not supported by statistics or nature, but this is what they believe. I believe that puberty leads to sex, like being shot in the head leads to dying. You can try to stop it, but you'll most often fail. In Switzerland there exists the world's most comprehensive sex education program. The Swiss also boast the lowest incidence of unplanned pregnancy and teen STDs on earth. Coincidence? I think not. Then there's the problem of gay folk. You don't have to be a fundamentalist to have a problem with homosexuality. It's been called "the last acceptable prejudice," and I see evidence that supports that assertion every day. All I can say is, gay people are out there. Gay kids are in your school, probably hiding, probably terrified, right now. Gay teens kill themselves 1300% more often than straight kids, because of the casual hate that we allow to flourish. It's just got to stop.

All that said, I hope you enjoy these plays. They are for staging, not just for reading. E-mail me about them (christopher_craddock@hotmail.com). My rates are always reasonable, and if you're a teen, hell, you can do them for free. Above all, teens, do plays. Write plays. Challenge your teachers. Debate with your parents. Think for yourself. Freedom is learned behaviour. Learn it and practise it. It is your privilege.

Chris Craddock
Edmonton, Alberta
November 2000

AZiMUTH THEATRE

PRESENTS

THE
DAY
BILLY
LIVED

BY CHRISTOPHER CRADDOCK

The Day Billy Lived

Production History

The Day Billy Lived was workshopped under the direction of Sophie Lees by Azimuth Theatre in November 1998.

Cast

Various	*Amy Berger*
The Man	*Irvin Munroe*
Secretary	*Elyne Quon*
Billy	*Jose Teodoro*
Various	*Richard Zyshley*
Dramaturge	*Joanna Falck*

The Day Billy Lived was first produced under the direction of Sophie Lees by Azimuth Theatre in February 1998.

Cast

Various	*Erin Malin*
Various	*Mark Meer*
The Man	*Irvin Munroe*
Secretary	*Vanessa Porteous*
Billy	*Jose Teodoro*
Designer	*Melinda Sutton*
Sound Design	*Darrin Hagen*
Stage Manager	*Erica Letchford*

Words and lyrics for the closing song were provided by Andy Northrup.

The Day Billy Lived was remounted under the direction of Sophie Lees by Azimuth Theatre in 1999.

Cast

Various	*Pru MacEvoy*
The Man	*Murray Utas*
Secretary	*Zoe Hawnt*
Billy	*Nathan Cuckow*
Various	*Josh Dean*

Designer	*Sarah Crooks*
Sound Design	*Dave Clarke*
Stage Manager	*Aaron Franks*
Road Manager	*Kerri Strobl*

The Characters
Billy: a boy, sixteen years old
Man: a metaphysical civil servant
Secretary: a metaphysical assistant
Rebecca: a disgruntled metaphysical civil servant
Mom: Billy's mother
Dad: Billy's father
Co-worker: a guy that Billy's Dad works with
Jennifer: a girl on a ledge
Amanda: Billy's friend
Joey: Billy's friend
Miss MacAllister: Billy's teacher
Monty: Not Billy's friend
Brenda: Billy's admirer
Billy: the Yuppie
Billy: the Lunatic
Billy: the Average

The Setting
The setting shifts from the main setting of an office to include many varied locations and thus the set needs to be versatile. The first production used a set of screens and a large metal box on wheels that served as both a desk and a bed.

Production Notes
The Day Billy Lived includes many topical and local references, and those mounting the play should feel absolutely free to change and update them, according to their specific social context. The play has many characters, but has always been done easily with as few as five actors. It's my opinion that it could also be done with as few as three actors, provided that they are amazing.

Billy sits in his room with his micro-tape recorder. He speaks into it.

Billy: Let me spell it out for you so there's no confusion later. The environment sucks. The government sucks. The future sucks. Everything sucks and I'm not going to take it anymore. I'm poisoning myself tonight! I have just taken one month's worth of prescription back pills and I must admit my back has never felt better. So you all can buy coke, and drain the rivers and burn the forests without me.

I'm outta here.
I'm leaving.
I'm going.
Good-bye.

Goodbye to my friends. You bunch of hooligans. You warped little freaks. You sludgy-faced bastards. I'll miss you.

Goodbye to Monica, but I guess we said our good-byes already. Too bad. I'm sure it would've been fun to be . . . friends.

And to my parents . . . well, I've never known what to say to my parents.

Pause.

Last Tuesday I stood on the library roof a good long time before deciding jumping wasn't for me. Last Friday I sat in the subway station three hours trying to work up the nerve. Last Sunday I took twenty-two Aspirin, had a nap on the couch and woke up with a headache. It's funny. A little will cure a headache, but too much, is just too much. Just like everything else. Look's like Dad's back pills are a winner, however, and I must admit my back has never felt better. Oh man, I already said that. *Small pause.* I want my room left just like it was. That's really important. I want it like a shrine. And I want a wax replica of me, sitting here, where I am, and I . . . want . . . I want . . . I want . . .

Billy passes out. Metaphysical servants emerge. They check his pulse and shake their heads. They form the office around him and arrange him in a chair. The Man enters and settles at the desk, shuffling papers distractedly. The Secretary putters about the office, gathering things, chattering to the Man, who largely ignores her.

Secretary: People are animals, more or less, eh dove?

Man: Animals—

Secretary: More or less, eh? Teeth and claws and drives and instincts. Quite good at being animals, if you come to think of it.

Man: I hadn't.

Secretary: Then do. Quite good at being animals. Much better than any of the others. That's why we're in charge.

Man: *Muttering.* These forms are . . .

Secretary: But then we have a few advantages to help us out. Opposable thumbs. Reason. And we've parlayed these advantages into world domination, despite the fact that lots of the other animals about could eat us. Well. That's no mean feat. Good for us then. We're smart.

Man: Good for us.

Secretary: We're in charge. We made up civilization. Malls and churches and taxes and cars. We did all that, cause we're so smart.

Man: Where did I put that . . .

Secretary: We invented discipline. We can overcome our instincts. We can overcome the urge to eat. Cookie?

Man: I'm on a diet.

Secretary: We can overcome the urge to mate. Dinner?

Man: *Looking up.* I'm on a diet.

Secretary: We can even override our self-preservation instinct. No other animals do that, do they? Except maybe lemmings, but that's just peer pressure for the most part. I think only humans complete suicide. But then you know that. That's why you're here, isn't it, ducky?

Man: Here I am.

Secretary: There you are. Animals, besides us, live until external circumstances dictate they can live no more. There are no housecat suicide hotlines. No goldfish therapy groups. No hamster crisis centres. Aren't they the healthy ones then? Maybe they should be running things, eh bearcub?

Man: *Finally choosing the papers he needs.* Maybe so.

Secretary: *Indicating Billy.* Do you want this one awake, then?

Man: If you would.

Secretary: Well, surely. Wake up then, chipmunk. Up and at 'em there . . . Move your eyes to open, chickadee! Shake off the dew you stinky monkey! Let's have it. C'mon. WAKE UP!

Billy: *Awaking suddenly.* Cripes!

Secretary: Anything more then, kittenfoot?

Man: That'll be everything. Thanks. So William, how are you?

Billy: *Looking around himself.* Fine . . .

Man: I see we have an application here for a self-initiated mortality.

Billy: For what?

Man: For a suicide. You've applied for a suicide?

Billy: Oh yeah. Yeah, that's right. I want a suicide.

Man: Uh huh. *Shuffles some papers.* A little young aren't you?

Billy: Sometimes it's better to wonder what you missed than to know.

Man: Heh, yeah, well I just have to ask for the form. You're a terminal case, right? In a lot of pain. Life reduced to watching machines blip, that kind of thing?

Billy: Everybody's life is reduced to watching machines blip.

Man: A cynic, huh? I guess I can't blame you. Listen, the regulations are clear for terminals. You just sign here and here and we'll get you on your way.

Billy: What do you mean by terminal?

Man: Your unbearable terminal disease.

Billy: I don't have a terminal disease. Since puberty cleared up, I feel pretty much okay. Physically.

Man: This isn't an unplug?

Billy: Unplug?

Man: This is a willful self-termination? You could have said something.

Billy: I don't even know what's going on.

Man: I don't have any of the right forms here.

Billy: Is this gonna take long? I was kinda hoping to walk towards a bright light.

Man: All in good time. Your application hasn't been processed yet.

Billy: Application? Bureaucracy? Even here?

Man: There are processes for everything. Do you know how many souls come in and out of here in a day?

Billy: I could care less. I took those pills to get away from stuff like this.

Man: Stuff like this could save your hide. You may yet decide you want to live. And with that dose you took, it could go either way.

Billy: I made my decision, man. I'm done. You got nothin' to say to change my mind.

Man: It's not my job to change your mind. Die, don't die. My coffee breaks come at the same time anyhow. It's my job to make you aware of the facts. You're a smart kid, you'll want to die informed. Besides, you haven't got a choice.

Billy: Sure I got a choice. I'll just get up and go.

Billy gets up to go. In a flash of sound and light he's passed out again with the secretary standing over him.

Secretary: Wake up then chipmunk. Up and at 'em there . . . Move your eyes to open, chickadee. Shake off the dew you stinky monkey. Let's have it. C'mon . . . WAKE UP!

Billy: *Awakening suddenly.* Cripes!

Secretary: Anything more, kittenfoot?

Billy: Wait a minute. Didn't we just do this?

Man: That's what happens when you try to leave. It gets real repetitive after a while.

Secretary: Did he try to leave?

Man: Yeah.

Secretary: I'll go reset the clocks. *Exits.*

Billy: I can't leave?

Man: No.

Billy: Christ.

Man: Not my department. You gonna sit still for this or what?

Billy: You are not going to change my mind.

Man: That's what they all say. May I do my job now?

Billy: I'll try and stay awake.

Man: I'll talk extra loud so it's easy. Let's start with the basics.

Man pulls down a screen with a man and a woman on it.

Man: Exhibit one. These are your parents. He's got some sperm. She's got some eggs. You with me so far?

Billy: It's dizzying, but I'll manage.

Man: So far, no big deal, right? Every guy's got sperm. Every girl's got eggs. But if you think it's no big deal you're missing the math of it. The statistics.

Billy: I hate math.

Man: Everybody does. But like Barney and fruitcake it's here to stay. Now see here. Your parents had parents, and their parents had parents too, and so on and so forth until the beginning of time. Now I have it on good information that your parents met at Wiarton Senior High. Dated for seven months before deciding to go all the way in the back of a '69 Chevy Duster. You were conceived, they were in love, or close enough, and they got married four months later. Your mother, slim woman that she was, was just beginning to show. Seventy-five thousand sperm vied for that egg, and of all of them, the best one made it and helped become you. Not just that but a thousand tiny factors that made your Mom drop her ice-cream cone on your Dad's foot outside the Mini Mart Choc'lit Shop. Not just that, but the thousand factors that made your Dad's family emigrate from Czechoslovakia to be in Canada at all, and not just that, but—

Billy: Are you going somewhere with this?

Man: The math of it, Billy. I got odds here that say a million to one. Hell, a billion to one that you should ever exist. That you should ever draw breath on this planet. Now maybe it's a divine plan and maybe it's dumb luck, but badda-bing, comin' atcha from a genetic crap shoot that's been goin' on forever and ever, a fully functional, walking, thinking, unique human. Billy DeVie! There you are.

Billy: Here I am.

Man: Against all odds.

Billy: I guess it does seem kind of unlikely when you lay it all out like that.

Man: Unlikely? Unlikely? It's unlikely that you'll win the lottery. It's unlikely you'll be struck by lightning. It's unlikely that Rhinos will march out of your butt and

crown you king of Rhinoland. This! That you're here!
That the primordial soup kicked up and spit out you,
just you, just the way you are—that's a miracle. And
a miracle's gotta be worth something, right?

Billy: I dunno from miracles, man—

Man: A billion to one. Hell, a trillion to one.

Billy: Yeah.

Man: So is it worth somethin' or not, Billy, waddaya say?

Billy: Sure.

Man: Man, this is like pulling teeth.

*Man pulls another screen down. It is in two parts. One marked
LIVE the other marked DIE. Man puts a mark on the LIVE side.*

Billy: What's that?

Man: Just keeping score.

*Enter Rebecca. She is efficient and somewhat intense. Some-
thing occurred between Man and Rebecca to make her very
tense with him, and him very apologetic with her.*

Rebecca: How's it coming?

Man: Hello Rebecca.

Rebecca: How's it coming?

Man: We just got started. William, this is Rebecca. She
works in spiritual repossession, up on the reincarna-
tion floor. Beck, this is Billy.

Billy: Hey.

Rebecca: *Giving Billy a cool looking over.* So, what's his problem? Is he checking out or what?

Man: We're still processing the application.

Rebecca: Still? What's the hold-up?

Man: These things take a little time, Beck.

Rebecca: Listen Willy—

Billy: Billy.

Rebecca: Whatever. I hate to see a soul like yours limited by unappreciative protoplasm. If you're not going to use it, I wish you'd hurry along so I can reassign.

Man: He's within his rights Beck.

Rebecca walks up to Billy and pulls something invisible and stretchy from Billy's chest.

Rebecca: You see that?

Billy: Not really.

Rebecca: That's prime, grade A soul. Makes for sensitive types, like you. It's capable of profound joy and profound suffering. You're too wrapped up in one to wait for the other. Your funeral. Soul like this, it's a gift and a burden. You gotta be tough to be happy, cause life can really suck. But if you don't have the guts, leave the soul for somebody who does.

Man: That's enough, Rebecca. Billy gets processing time, just like everybody else.

Billy: He's holding up the show, not me.

Rebecca: *Smiling.* I'll be seeing you.

Exits.

Billy: That was severe.

Man: She takes her job very seriously. Anyway, back to the carnival.

Billy: Hold up. She wanted my soul?

Man: Can you blame her? It's the best soul I've seen this month. Big. Generous. A streak of the artistic with just a hint of melancholy. People wait in line weeks for a soul like that upstairs. If we can make you feel a bit better and put it to work painting pictures and curing cancer, we might really have something there.

Man gives Billy's soul a tug, stretching it out in front of his face. Billy stares a moment. Man lets it snap back, rocking Billy in his seat.

Man: I have some literature on what you'd miss. Certain movies already in production for 2000. The new Spice Girl. But if you're that set on going out, a film version of Spiderman isn't going to change your mind.

Billy: Red costume or black?

Man: Now that doesn't really matter to you, does it?

Billy: Nah. No way.

Man: Yeah. But what about this?

A pantomime of Billy's mother finding Billy's body. She knocks on the door to call him for supper. She sees Billy on the chair. She nudges him good naturedly. He slips to the floor. She kneels beside him and shakes him with growing panic. She grabs him up in her arms, holding his head to her chest, sobbing and rocking the body.

Man: That's about how your Mom will react, huh?

Billy: *Shaken.* So what. She'll get over it. She deserves it.

Man: She does?

Billy: Yeah. She never reads the paper, and—and she makes me go to church and she's always trying to get me to eat meat. She's stupid.

Man: Moms can be difficult, I grant you. But she loves you right?

Billy: It's always, "Turn down that Satan music," and "Say the blessing" at dinner, and she has no respect for my own integrity, my, my own thoughts and—

Man: Is this all about her?

Billy: It's not just her—

Man: It's bound to be kinda tough on her, though, huh?

Billy: Get away with this guilt trip, man.

Man: No trip. Just the truth. Everything has consequences for everything else.

Billy: That's why I'm out of here, man, to—

Man: To avoid the consequences. But they happen anyway, right? Just without you.

Billy: Yeah. I won't be here, so they can just do what they do and that's it.

Man: That's it.

Billy: Yeah.

Man: You're a socially conscious guy, right? That's part of why we're here. The environment and that.

Billy: Yeah, so—

Man: So what's the big difference between leaving radio-active stuff around and messing everything up and leaving emotional stuff around and messing everything up.

Billy: Yeah, well. You can't make an omelet without breaking a few eggs.

Man: And besides, she deserves it, right?

Billy: Well, you know what I mean. It's not like she's horrible.

Man: No. In fact, according to the information I have, she's within her rights.

Billy: Her rights?

Man: Let's see, it's around here somewhere. Ah. The rights of Mom. Moms can be sarcastic. Can object to foul language and loud music. Can dress you funny, up to a certain age, it varies from culture to culture. You know in Lithuania, Moms are allowed to—

Billy: You don't know my parents, man.

Man: "Parents." They can be great. They can be your friends. True, usually not until you move out, but until then they can be great people to get to know.

Billy: It's not Mom so much. It's the father figure.

Man: Yeah. I got the file on that.

Billy: Yeah.

Man: What can I say, Billy. Except fight back.

Billy: Right. And get killed.

Man: Not like that. Defend yourself within yourself. Get some help where you can as well. If not your Mom, maybe there's a cool teacher or uncle or somebody like that you could talk to. I know it's hard to believe from where you're sitting, but not all adults are out to get you.

Billy: Huh.

Man: If you let him drive you to this, who loses?

Billy: At least he'd know. For once, he'd know.

Man: Your father had a father. And maybe what your father is now is about what his father did. That's not your problem. Your problem is getting safe. And to learn to be maybe a little different if you ever decide to become a Dad yourself. Abuse, abuse, abuse . . . no abuse. It doesn't have to be the family heirloom. You're the guy to stop it. That's your job.

Billy: I just don't know if I'm up to it.

Man: I'm not saying it's easy. You know, this might be hard to swallow. But your Dad, despite everything, he loves you. He's proud of you.

Billy: Right. And I'm Dennis Rodman.

Man: I have proof.

Billy's Dad enters in a hard hat, carrying a card. A co-worker approaches.

Co-worker: You gonna get up on that crane, Roy?

Dad: Yeah, in a second. You see this? It's Billy's report card.

Co-worker: Safe to say he doesn't get it from you.

Dad: You ain't kiddin'. His Mom was real smart in school, though. Even chemistry. I could never do chemistry.

Co-worker: You gonna hang it in your locker with the other ones?

Dad: What's it to you?

Co-worker: Nothin' Ray. You gonna get up on that crane, now?

Dad: Yeah. *Folds the card and puts it in his breast pocket.* Yeah, right with ya.

Back to office with Man and Billy.

Man: So what do you think of that?

Billy: Who the hell are you? What is this? How do you know all this?

Man: Somebody's got to know everything.

Billy: So, what . . . you're . . . God?

Man: Not my department.

Billy: Look, it's real sweet that my Dad likes me more than I thought, okay, but there is nothing out there. There are no jobs, there's gonna be no air, the ice caps are gonna melt and then there'll be no land. The earth is so messed up. Western civilization is just over.

Man: I know it's bad.

Billy: Bad and getting worse.

Man: Maybe you could join Greenpeace or—

Billy: No, you—

Man: What?

Billy: You try to make everything sound easy. Well it's not. It's not easy.

The Secretary enters with an accordian folder.

Billy: The future is like this big black whirlpool and we're all getting sucked into it.

Secretary: The future?

Billy: What?

Secretary: Pardon, woodchuck, but are you talking about the future?

Billy: Yeah—to him.

Secretary: Are you saying you know what's going to happen?

Billy: The same thing that always happens. Nothing.

Secretary: You're saying you can actually see your future?

Billy: That's what I'm saying. I can see my whole life, and it sucks.

Secretary: Such wisdom in such a young one. You amaze me. Oops. *Dropping a pen.* Could you get that?

Billy does. While he's bent over, the Secretary smacks him in the back of the head.

Billy: Ow!

Secretary: Oh I'm sorry. Stand up.

Billy does.

Secretary: Have a chocolate.

She pops a chocolate into his mouth.

Secretary: Isn't that good?

Billy: Mm hmm!

Secretary: Then do a little dance.

She spins Billy around. Then she stomps on Billy's foot.

Billy: Ow!

Secretary: Sorry.

She kisses Billy on the mouth.

Billy falls back into his chair.

Secretary crosses to the door.

Secretary: Did you know all that was gonna happen?

Billy: No . . .

Secretary: Oh. Well I guess you can't see the future after all. You want some coffee then, my woodchuck?

Man: I'm fine.

Secretary: Alrighty, then.

Billy: Is it hard to get a job here?

Secretary: The hours suck, but the pay is terrible. Well, back to work. *Exits.*

Billy: Can't I die yet?

Man: You're proving to be a challenge.

Billy: I thought you might appreciate my determination.

Man: It does take determination to kill yourself. But it takes more determination to live.

Billy: Where did you get a line like that?

Man: Um. From this pamphlet here.

Billy: Pamphlets? You're grasping at straws, man.

Man: I have a few tricks up my sleeve.

Billy: Yeah? Like what?

Man: Field trip!

In a flash they are on a ledge of a very tall building. Billy immediately reacts to the height. The Man stands casually. A little away from them is a woman fixing to jump.

Billy: WOAH! Oh man.

Murray Utas as Man, Nathan Cuckow as Billy, and Pru MacEvoy as Jennifer.
PHOTO BY BRYAN'S PHOTOGRAPHY.

Man: This is Jennifer. This is a ledge. Way down there is the ground.

Billy: I do not like heights, man.

Man: Neither does Jennifer.

Billy: No, I do not like heights at all man. They freak me right out.

Man: Well, you're going in. Talk to her. You will be visible in five, four, three . . .

Man mouths the two, one, and points at Billy. Billy becomes visible to Jennifer who screams. Billy screams too and nearly falls.

Jennifer: Where did you come from?

Billy: Leduc.

Jennifer: No, just now.

Billy: It's a long story. Listen, do you know a good way to get inside?

Jennifer: Don't you try to stop me. Don't you dare. I'll jump. I'll jump right now.

Man: Don't let her do that.

Billy: You can't do that.

Jennifer: Don't you tell me. I decide what I can and can't do. Don't you tell me.

Man: You better come up with something.

Billy: Like what?

Man: I'm just a civil servant.

Jennifer: What is your problem?

Billy: I don't know what I'm doing.

Jennifer: That's obvious.

Billy: *To Man.* Can't you help me out?

Man: You're on your own.

Jennifer: Help you out? Fine. First you start with non-judgmental listening. Then be sure to affirm my feelings by taking me seriously. Never accuse me of attention-seeking. Then show and describe your caring to me, by—

Billy: I think we're beyond all that.

Jennifer: I think so too.

Billy: So. So give me ten good reasons you should jump off this building.

Man: Oh geez.

Jennifer: What?

Billy: It's a big decision. You don't make a decision this big without ten good reasons.

Jennifer: Don't play games with me.

Billy: I'm not. I just want to know what a young, beautiful woman like you wants to jump off a perfectly good building for.

Jennifer: Don't call me that. Don't call me beautiful.

Billy: Come on. Just ten. Ten good reasons.

Pause.

Jennifer: Because life is stupid and pointless. Because I'm never going to be anyone or anything. Because nobody cares anyway.

Billy: Uh huh. That's just three, Jennifer. That's not enough, okay. That's not enough reasons. Give me some more.

Jennifer: Because. Oh God, I don't know.

Billy: C'mon Jennifer. You can do it. Just seven more.

Jennifer: Because the new fall fashions are ugly.

Billy: *Laughs.* That's four.

Jennifer: Because there's nothing good on TV.

Billy: I can't accept that last one.

Jennifer: What?

Billy: What about *The Simpsons*, huh? It's a cool show.

Jennifer: *The Simpsons?*

Billy: Well, it's a pretty cool show, right?

Jennifer: *Confused.* Yeah.

Billy: So don't you want to see next season?

Jennifer: I missed a bunch because of my job. I wouldn't even know what was going on. Forget it.

Billy: That's the beauty of *The Simpsons*. Every time they just start back at the beginning. You don't have to know anything.

Jennifer: I wish I could start over.

Billy: You can—

Jennifer looks down and shakes her head.

Billy: Look, even if everything else looks really bad, there's still *The Simpsons*, right? There's still one or two good things. Even on TV. Right? Jennifer? Right?

Pause.

Jennifer: You seem nice. But it's too much. Everything. It's just too much.

Billy: Jennifer, look. Don't do this, okay. There is stuff for someone like you. There's Spring and walks and renting roller blades and—

Jennifer: Bye.

Billy: Jennifer. JENNIFER!

Back in the office.

Billy: We're back? Oh man, did she jump? What happened?

Man: People's ends are their own. We're not a tabloid.

Billy: What was she even doing up there?

Man: You tell me, Billy.

Billy: She was not like me, okay? She was pretty and, and funny, the new fall fashions are ugly, and she was up there to—

Man: She was a lot like you.

Billy: No way. She had a lot going on, I could tell, you know—

Man: Yeah, she did. She had a lot going on and she was pretty and funny and she didn't think so. She thought she was bad and so was everything else. She was just like you.

Billy: She was not like me.

Man: You don't always have the perspective on yourself that other people have on you.

Billy: What do you know about what people think of me?

Man: We have unsolicited testimony.

Billy: You have what?

Man: Just watch.

Amanda enters.

Amanda: Billy's cool. He can ollie[1] really big and he went to BC to protest them cutting down trees. A bunch of us were gonna go, but we were scared of being put in jail. But Billy went anyway and he didn't get put in jail cause he was only there for like forty-five minutes on the way to Vancouver to visit his uncle with the hemorrhoids. But he still went, and I think that rocks! He knows about indy[2] bands and he helped me get an e-mail address and that stuff is like, beyond me, like computers, WAH, but Billy knows that stuff, cause he's got a head for knowin'. He's a smartie. And a sweetie. A smartie-sweetie. Okay that sounded dumb.

Joey enters.

Joey: Billy saved me once. This big ugly skater guy wanted my head, cause I said that Green Day was a weenie band. This skater guy was way bigger than me and a little bigger than Billy but Billy stood his ground. He walked right up to that skater and looked him in the eye and said, "Hey man. He was just kidding. Don't be mad. Please?" And then the skater guy punched him, and Billy bled, well . . . he bled for a long time. But then the skater guy went away, so Billy saved my bacon, totally! I'd like to return the favor, but I need my nose to work right cause . . . I play bagpipes.

Miss MacAllister enters.

Miss MacAllister: Billy is one of my favourites. It's true that you're not really supposed to pick favorites, but every teacher does and Billy is one of mine as well as Greg and Maxwell. He wrote this story, Billy did, about a sapling and his parents are trees next to him, but they get clear cut, and the sapling has to grow up alone. It just touched me so, and had excellent punctuation. So I made a photocopy and I keep it in this scrapbook that I have of beautiful poems and leaves and bits of material and newspaper clippings about giantism.

Monty enters.

Monty: Billy is the best offensive guard in the high school league! And big? Fergetaboutit! His arms are like big . . . arms. His arms are like his legs and his legs are . . . big. He hits so hard, Fergetaboutit. Like a truck, he hits—and . . . Billy DeVie? I thought you were talking about Billy Meyers. . . . I don't even know Billy DeVie. . . . Oh the tree-hugger kid? No. I don't know that guy. But isn't he kinda . . . small?

Brenda enters.

Brenda: I don't know that Billy knows me, but I know him and I think he's really cute. Not that he's a Gap ad or anything, but he just has . . . really deep eyes. And I hear about his environmental protests and I just want to eat him up. Just wanna go and fight the good fight by his side, like a Kennedy or something. And I heard how Monica dumped him and she is just so stupid because Billy was way too good for her and she has bad hair. I, heh, I wrote a song for him. For Billy. But don't tell him. Unless he lets on that he likes me, then you can say that I think he's cute, but you can't tell about the song, cause he'll think, like, *psycho sounds* REEEE REEEEEE, and I'd hate for him to think that. It goes, "How do I say this without sounding gushy. I'm afraid if he hears this it might come out mushy." Heh. I'm still working on it.

Back to the office.

Man: Huh? Surprised?

Billy: Brenda MacPherson wrote me a song.

Man: These people think you're kinda special.

Billy: I didn't know she could write songs.

Man: People are wacky, huh?

Billy: Yeah. Wacky.

Man: You never know what they're gonna do, and it's kinda fun to watch them do it. People are like snowflakes, no two alike and there's six billion of them to get to know. I think "LIVE" gets another point here.

Billy: Brenda wrote me a song. Huh.

Man: I'll take that as a yes. *Makes a mark.* It's two nothin' Billy.

Billy: I work best under pressure.

Man: This isn't a game, Billy.

Billy: You're keeping score, aren't you?

Man: There is a lot at stake here!

Billy: I know that.

Man: I'm your last chance.

Billy: What did I just say?

Man: Billy, you have to understand—

Billy: SHUT UP A MINUTE!

The Man freezes. Billy faces the audience.

Billy: I'm lying. I'm lying to you. It's not the environment or government conspiracy or that. I mean that stuff's bad and something's got to be done, but it's not that, for me. It's that . . . I got this little ball of pain. Here. And I don't know exactly what it's about or how it got there, but it's there. And it gets bigger as I go. And as I go, it gets harder to get on with things. And the ball just seems to suck the stuff out of what I do. Sucks the meaning, the joy. Sucks the fun right out of everything I try to do. And I'm scared. I'm so scared it'll just get bigger and bigger. . . . If I was just a little stronger, a better person, maybe I could take the ball. Look at it. Try to figure out something to do about it, but, but I'm weak. I know that I am, and I don't really want to go, you know, to die. But all I can see is everything getting worse and me getting worse and there's that ball, that STUPID ball sucking at everything. And I don't know what to do about it. I don't know what to do.

Man: —that I'm trying to help.

Billy: I'm right here.

Man: You really got me stumped. Usually this is a last resort kind of thing, but—

Billy: But?

Man: It's time for possible futures.

Billy: Possible futures?

Man: You know those Freedom 55 commercials, people run into themselves when they're older?

Billy: Yeah?

Man: It's like that. Check it out.

A series of Later Time Billys.

Yuppie Billy: Well, hi there. I'm William DeVie, forty-five
years old and married to the happiest little home-
maker you ever did see. I work in the environmental
industry. And believe you me, it IS an industry. I
made those commercials with Marlon Brando and
the sperm whales. Yes those are mine. Heh heh . . . I
play golf. . . . Yes I do. . . . So is this for TV or what?
How's my hair?

Mentally Ill Billy: Fooled you, didn't I? I seem like a perfectly normal human being, don't I? FOOLED YOU!
HA HAHAHA HA! A closer examination would reveal
that I am not a human at all, but a complex vehicle
made of cloned human flesh. And in my head is a
tiny alien, pulling levers to control these arms and
legs! BEHOLD! *Moves arms and legs.* Quite a trick is it
not? Were you not fooled completely? Yesyouwere—
ofcourseyouwere. I think such a trick as that deserves
. . . some spare change! Spare change? Every little bit
helps. Thank you puny human. Spare change?

Average Billy: Hey. I'm Billy. Or Bill. Or William.
Whatever. I work as an usher at the movie theatre
down the way. Been there a coupla years. I'm thinking of something different. Maybe a video store . . .
maybe. Me and Brenda moved in together. If you
missed our housewarming, you missed out cause it
rocked, ha. It was fun. Brenda's a musician, she plays
guitar in coffee shops and at the mall. She's great.
She wrote me this song, "How do I say this without
sounding mushy . . . ?" She's still working on it.
She's always working on it. This one time she sang

in this coffee shop where one of my paintings was hanging up. It was so cool. Her playing. My painting. Her. Me. . . . Us. . . . Usually at this point in the dream the dancing dwarf comes out.

Back to the office.

Billy: Whoah. Who was that middle guy?

Man: You. And the first guy, and the last guy. All of them, possible yous.

Billy: I didn't find the middle guy especially encouraging.

Man: Well I beg your pardon, but I never promised you a rose garden. If you're waiting for me to say, Go! Live! and it'll be all bubble baths and beautiful girls, don't wait no more. One of those guys could be you or none of 'em. All I'm selling is a second chance. You might get famous, you might get fat and bald, but you won't get to be anything if you don't hop back up on the Lifecycle.

Billy: Lifecycle?

Man: For us it's material existence, for you it's an exercise bike. So sue me.

Rebecca bursts in with a high caliber pistol.

Rebecca: The buck stops here.

Man: Beck, what are you doing?

Rebecca: *Loading the gun.* Wait. Wait. Wait. That's all I do. Wait around while an endless supply of whiny wankers decide if they want to throw it away or not. I'm tired of it.

Man: Rebecca, put down the gun. This is dangerous and against regulations.

Rebecca: So Billy. You wanna die. That's the point, right? The reason we're all here?

Man: Is this about the other night, Beck, cause I can explain—

Rebecca: I mean what do you want?

Billy: Rebecca—Can I call you Rebecca?

Rebecca: We give you Spring days, newborn babies, an animated Batman series—

Man: Don't do this Rebecca!

Rebecca: *Puts the gun to Billy's forehead.* And still you come to us. And we have to wheedle you into a commitment to a perfectly good life. *Cocks the gun.*

Billy: Oh Geez.

Rebecca: I know you have problems. We all have problems. But the universe is doing its best. Now I'm tired of the arguing. We're gonna finish this here and now. *Hands him the gun.* Here it is. No pills. No drifting off into a pleasant, permanent sleep. Here's a GUN. So do it right now or don't do it at all. What's it gonna be Billy? . . . Are you gonna live or are you gonna die?

Man snaps his fingers and Rebecca freezes. Man takes her gun and puts it on the desk.

Man: Give me a hand, here, wouldya?

Metaphysical servants come and carry the still frozen Rebecca off.

Man: Now, where were we?

Billy picks up the gun and levels it at Man.

Billy: Okay. I'm sorry about this. I thank you for your time, but I need to get on with my afterlife. Now.

Man: No can do, pal. You're just going to have to shoot me.

Billy: What is it with you people?

Man: Just not in the face, okay? I've got a date later.

Billy: I am not kidding around here.

Man: *Mockingly.* I'm not kidding around here—just shoot me.

Billy: You're crazy.

Man: Shoot me. SHOOT ME! What is the trigger stuck? Is it too tight? Do you need help?

Billy: Back the hell off, man!

Man: Why? What are you going to do? Shoot me? So SHOOT ME!

Billy shoots the ceiling. There should be a loud bang, but flowers come out of the barrel of the gun. Billy is scared by the noise and doesn't realize the flowers are there for a moment. He does, and then slumps in his chair.

Man: Now don't you feel foolish?

Billy: Yes.

Man: Good. Now where were we?

Billy: Just finished off with the possible futures.

Man: Right. Oh, quick question first. What was your answer?

Billy: What?

Man: For Rebecca. You want to live, you want to die. I mean, all the pressure with the gun and all, what was your first thought?

Pause.

Man: Well, I guess the answer is in there somewhere. Listen Billy, this question isn't on the form, but I gotta ask. What do you need up there? Like if I could make everything just like you'd like it to keep on keepin' on up there, what would it be like?

Billy: Geez. I don't know.

Cheezy TV music wafts in.

Billy: Mom! Dad! I'm home!

Mom: Hello, son!

Dad: Hey there big guy! Did you drive the water powered car or the solar moped home?

Billy: I took one of the city's teleportation devices. They're quick and there's no noise pollution.

Dad: Can't beat public transportation.

Billy: How was your day?

Mom: I made vegetarian lasagna!

Billy: My favourite!

Dad: And I sorted your fan mail. I tell you, being the lead singer for a political-environmental band that still manages to stay on the forefront of popular music sure nets you a lot of mail.

Mom: Not that we mind.

Dad: Not a bit. We're real proud of you son.

Mom: Really proud and full of love.

Dad: Your Mom said it for the both of us. How was your day?

Billy: I had lunch with the Pope. He's decided to ordain women and gays on my advice!

Mom: Well that's just super!

Billy: And then we had a showdown, playing in turn our electric guitars on national TV!

Dad: How'd you do?

Billy: Well, the Holy Father plays a mean ax.[3]

Dad: But?

Billy: But you know I can't be beat.

Dad: HA ha. I sure do, son.

Mom: You'd better spend some time with Flipper before dinner. Having a friend dolphin is a big responsibility.

Billy: *Moving to a window.* EEEEE EEEEEE EEEE AHHH AHHH!

Off. EEEEH EEEH!

Dad: That crazy, thinking fish! He sure loves you.

Mom: And so do I, son.

Dad: Your Mom said it for the both of us.

Ding dong!

Dad: Now who could that be?

Mom: Why, it's Monica!

Monica: I was so wrong Billy. And you were so right. Let's never break up again.

Billy: Here's lookin' at you kid.

Mom: Oh my goodness look at the time.

Dad: You'll be late for your sold-out concert!

Mom: Better teleport right away!

Dad: Rock out, son.

Mom: Do a stage dive for me!

Billy: This one's for you. The best girlfriend and parents an environmentalist rock star could have.

Billy is enveloped by his loving crowd. Screams and guitars ring out.

Back at the office.

Man: You don't ask for much, do you?

Billy: Well, it is a best-case scenario.

Man: It certainly is. Nobody's life is that good. But everybody's got to do their best with what they've got.

Billy: And what have I got?

Man: You got a lot more than most people. I'm not sayin' it makes your life a bed of roses, but you have got a place to live. Food to eat. Reasonable surety a bomb isn't gonna fall on your house while you're at the mall.

Billy: We are the world. We are the children.

Man: I'm not saying you have to live in Grozny to get depressed, but I do have a point, right? You are not starving. You are not war torn. You are not the object of ethnic cleansing.

Billy: Just draw the little line, man.

Man: I believe I will.

Puts another mark on the LIVE side. The Secretary enters and putters subtly.

Man: We're making progress then. I've gotten you to admit your life is not the worst of all possible situations.

Billy: Well that's just it, isn't it? We got cell phones, microwave ovens, and so much food we have to puke to stay thin. We got Disney, malls, and free health care. We got all this stuff. We got it better than anyone else, this is as good as it gets in the whole world, and I STILL feel like hell. I mean, there's probably nothing great about being dead, but what is so great about being alive?

Secretary: Things that are great about being alive. Well, let me see. There's brushing your hair with a big soft brush. Having your feet rubbed. Getting a haircut. Picking your nose when there's no one about and you can really dig. Watching *Star Wars*. Being too hot at night and finding the fresh, cool spot in the sheets. Something yummy coming out of the oven. A long, firm bowel movement. Hearing wind in the trees. Having genitals and all that goes with them. There's floating in calm water. Scratching a mosquito bite. Meeting a famous person. Peeing, after being in the car a long time. The sight of someone really hot coming your way. Eating Dip and Lik candy. Sitting by an ocean and getting a small glimpse of forever, and knowing that somehow, no one is alone. . . . I brought you your coffee.

Billy: He didn't want any coffee.

Secretary: Oh, that's right. Aren't I the billygoat, then? Well, take care, sparrow. *Exits.*

Billy: *Admiring.* Who is that woman?

Man: Well what have we here? It's three nothing. Confidentially, Billy, I have never lost at three nothing.

Billy: Never, huh?

Man: Not even one time.

Billy: Well. Let me tie it up for you.

Billy takes the marker and makes a line for every point he makes.

Billy: People can be cruel and irresponsible. Life can seem pointless and absurd. It's really, really, hard to make a difference in the world. There. Three all.

Man: Three all.

Billy: You should never say never. Not in your position.

Man: Oh Billy—

Billy: Three all. But you know what?

Man: What?

Billy: I'm gonna live anyway.

Man: Say again?

Billy: I'm gonna live anyway. I'm gonna rent *Star Wars*, I'm gonna—eat ice cream. I'm gonna—I'm gonna live anyway.

Brenda MacPherson appears. She begins to sing the Billy song, in a clean, polished, musical theatre fashion.

Brenda: How do I say this without sounding gushy . . .
     I'm scared if he hears this, it might come out mushy.
     But the likelihood is I'm the only one who'll know . . .

The conclusion of The Day Billy Lived.
PHOTO BY BRYAN'S PHOTOGRAPHY.

. . . And so . . .
Billy is the kind guy who makes people listen.
There's something in his eyes to indicate he's got
        vision.
He's got a heart that's deep and true.
And even though he still gets blue.
It's just because the world keeps letting him down.

Billy: What's going on?

Man: It's the universe celebrating. Just go with it.

Brenda: *Singing.* Billy takes the time to understand what
        he's feeling.
I've seen him lost in space and I've peeled him off
        the ceiling.
He's got an artist in his soul,
And I can't see him getting old.
If he could only see what I've always seen in him.
Billy, the world needs more like you.
Billy, I wish I were more like you.
Billy, please don't feel like you're alone.
Billy, I want the best for you.
Billy, the world's a test for you.
Billy, let's live our lives close to the bone.

Billy: Oh Geez. Do we have to?

Man: I'm afraid so.

They join in, somehow completely aware of the choreography.

Billy, the world needs more like you.
Billy, I wish there were more like you.
Billy, please just don't feel that you're alone.
Billy, I want the best for you.
Billy, the world's a test for you.
Billy, let's live our lives close to the bone.

The last line repeats dreamily. Brenda et al *exit. Billy collapses at his desk in the position he took at the top of the show. He jerks awake. He feels suddenly nauseous and throws up into a wastepaper basket.*

Mom: *Off.* Billy? Goodness Billy are you okay in there?

Billy: Yeah, Mom. Yeah. I'll be okay. . . . Mom? Could we . . . umm. Mom, could we . . . talk?

Notes:
[1] The little hop that skateboarders do up onto a curb or rail.
[2] Short for "independent."
[3] Colloquial term for guitar.

Azimuth
Theatre
presents

Winter
tour 2006

Wrecked

by Christopher Craddock

directed by Sophie Lees

Wrecked

Production History

Wrecked was workshopped under the direction of Sophie Lees by Azimuth Theatre in December 1999.

Cast

Lyle	*Chris Bullough*
Sharon	*Liana Shannon*
Bartender / Buddy	*Murray Utas*
Susy	*Daniela Vlaskalic*

All actors play various teens in the TEEN SCENES as appropriate.

Wrecked was produced under the direction of Sophie Lees by Azimuth Theatre in February 2000.

Cast

Lyle	*Chris Bollough*
Sharon	*Liana Shannon*
Bartender / Buddy	*Murray Utas*
Susy	*Beth Graham*

Designer	*Marrissa Kochanski*
Costume Design	*Kate Connell Banigan*
Sound Design	*Dave Clarke*
Stage / Road Manager	*Siobahn Pettigrew*

All actors play various teens in the TEEN SCENES as appropriate.

The Characters

Lyle: a boy, sixteen
Buddy: his friend, sixteen
Susy: Lyle's sister, ten
Sharon: Lyle and Susy's mother, thirty-five
The Bartender: a bartender, thirty-three
Teen One
Teen Two
Teen Three
Teen Four
AA Members One, Two and Three

Production Notes

The setting of the production moves quickly from place to place, so the set needs to be versatile. The teen scenes are intended to show slices of life within the high school community that surrounds the main characters, and none of the characters in the teen scenes mentioned by name impacts directly on the main plot or characters. Feel free to add local references wherever appropriate and to update any references to elements of popular culture.

THE TEENS

The teens line up.

One: Last night I got so drunk.

Two: Wasted?

Three: Pissed.

Four: How pissed?

One: Wrecked. I had this mix from my parents' liquor cabinet. You've seen my parents' liquor cabinet.

Two: Nice liquor cabinet.

One: Exactly. So I got an ounce of this, an ounce of that, like fourteen ounces of hard alcohol all mixed up in my coke slurpee. I am set and the party is jumping.

Two: I was at that party.

Three: Good party.

Four: Fine party.

One: Great party. And pretty soon I see Sharlene.

Three: Hi!

One: Hi! . . . and she is just as drunk as I am.

Two: Pissed?

One: Wasted.

Four: And I was really pissed, but even still, when he hit me, it hurt. But then, I hit him back and he went down hard . . . partly . . . cause he was so pissed, and he hit his head on the stereo, which broke . . . his head AND the stereo . . . and he needed stitches, so, hey . . . you know . . . I won the fight.

The teens: Chris Bullough, Beth Graham, and Murray Utas.
PHOTO BY SOPHIE LEES.

One: And since I was pissed and Sharlene was pissed, we, uh, got together, you know what I'm saying, it was all friendly. I think you know what I mean.

Three: When I get drunk . . . I just—I was gonna wait. At least until he bought me dinner or something. But I was drunk, so . . .

Two: So, I had puked a lot in the past. I mean, there is usually a certain amount of puking, but this was a lot of puking even for me, on account of the mickey of vodka I pounded and we had done the drive-through and I had the two cheeseburger meal. So I puked and puked and this was only like eight o'clock so when eleven came around and everybody else had to puke I was already passed out with my head in the can. Everybody else had to puke in the flower garden.

Three: Oh my God.

One: And then the cops came.

Two: The cops.

Four: My parents are going to kill me.

One: Hello?

Three: Hi. It's Sharlene.

One: Hi!

Two: So then the cops came, and everybody wanted to get in the bathroom, cause tons of people had dope and they all wanted to flush it down the toilet. But I was puking and all and I had the door locked, so . . . some guys got busted. That's what I heard, anyhow.

One: What's the matter?

Three: I think I'm pregnant.

One: Oh my god.

Pause.

Buddy is setting up a camera on a tripod. He is dressed in a fatsuit and a scraggly wig. He looks like a clown drunk.

Buddy: Okay. It's up. You ready?

Lyle: Yeah, I'm ready. Hit record and get outta frame.

Buddy: You remember what to say?

Lyle: Yeah, I remember what to say.

Buddy: I'm hitting record. You're ready?

Lyle: Yeah. Are you ready?

Buddy: I'm ready. Are you ready?

Lyle: I'm ready.

Buddy: You're ready?

Lyle: I'm so ready.

Buddy: Then we're goin'.

Lyle: Let's go.

Buddy: Oh—Just a second . . . *He takes off the lens cap.*

Lyle: Are you high?

Buddy: Um . . . no.

Lyle: We said no smoking while we work on the thing.

Buddy: Dude! I haven't smoked at all today.

Lyle: Buddy?

Buddy: Okay, I smoked a little roach, so what?

Lyle: Buddy—Whatever. As long as you're ready.

Buddy: I'm ready. Are you ready?

Lyle: I'm ready.

Buddy: You're ready?

Lyle: I'm so ready.

Buddy: Then we're goin'.

Lyle: Let's go.

Buddy: Go.

Lyle: *Lyle turns to the camera.* When you've got a drunk at your house, it's a little like having a monster to take care of. Some are like werewolves and some are like Frankensteins, but most are monsters nobody ever made a movie about. They look just like humans and lead basically human lives. The difference is this: they are addicted to a potion. And it's the potion that transforms them. Let's run down the basic types so you can be prepared for their care and feeding.

Buddy comes out in an angry pose and freezes.

There's the Brute. Note the angry expression and the veins popping out of the neck and forehead. He or she is usually characterized by a loud voice and the shouting of things. It might sound like this:

Buddy: I'm the only one pulling my weight around here!

Lyle: Or like this:

Buddy: You people are all against me!

Lyle: Or sometimes:

Buddy: Jeez—you dumb—I oughta . . . then you'd see what . . . oh geez I fell down.

Lyle: Sometimes the brute won't be satisfied with just shouting. He might move to hitting. Most people cope with that, by hiding. Some good hiding places are: under the bed, up a tree, or if you have the grades, college. Then there's Mr. or Mrs. Weepy. Note the sad, bleary eyes. They sometimes sound a bit like this:

Buddy: I've made a lot of mistakes in my time.

Lyle: Or this:

Buddy: Hey where you going?

Lyle: Or this:

Buddy: Jeez—you dumb—I oughta . . . then you'd see what . . . oh geez I fell down.

Lyle: There's Mr. Pukey, The Sex Machine, The Sleeper, Mr. Shouty, Johnny-I-Know-all-about-the-War-in-the-Middle-East, and my personal favourite The Psycho. But I think you get the picture. There's a lot of kinds of drunks in the world. In fact, it can happen to any-body. So if your Mom or Dad is a lousy drunk, get some help. Before you fall into the wrong crowd, or ruin your marks or get a really embarrassing tattoo. And don't start drinking yourself. Or you might end up just like them. A lousy drunk.

Buddy: A message from "Moms against Teen Drinking."

Pause.

Lyle: And . . . cut.

Buddy: Not bad.

Lyle: Pretty good.

Buddy: Best yet.

Lyle: I agree.

Buddy: Do you think it'll win the contest?

Lyle: We gotta edit it, and add music and—

Buddy: Yeah, yeah, I know, but after that, do you think it'll win?

Lyle: I don't know.

Buddy: Hey. If we win and it goes on TV and—

Lyle: And we get the prize money.

Buddy: Five grand!

Lyle: Five grand.

Buddy: But—won't your Mom be pissed?

Lyle: What?

Buddy: Like mad at you. About the commercial.

Lyle: Why?

Buddy: Well . . . the commercial is totally harsh about alcoholics.

Lyle: Yeah?

Buddy: And your Mom is totally . . . a . . .

Lyle: . . . a what?

Buddy: . . . Nothing.

Lyle: Good.

Buddy: I bet she gets mad, though.

Lyle: Why?

Buddy: . . . For no reason at all.

Susy enters.

Susy: There was this movie I saw once. It was about this
snowy town at the bottom of a bunch of snowy
mountains. And the people in the town had to be
careful all the time, because if they made too much
noise or too many vibrations, the snow would come
avalanching down on them. And they'd be buried
and gone. Forever. . . . That's what it's like at my
house. You can't make too many vibrations. My
Mom is like a whole bunch of snow, sometimes. And
sometimes, I'm afraid of her. I guess that's silly
though. To be afraid of your Mom. Everybody else I
know is afraid of their Dad.

Lyle gets home.

Susy: Hi.

Lyle: Hi. Have you seen my walkman?

Susy: I ate it.

Lyle: You ate it.

Susy: I ate it and then I puked it up and then I flushed it
so it's gone.

Lyle: Yeah okay, that's hilarious, so where's my walkman?

Susy: Some Martians came.

Lyle: Martians.

Susy: Some Martians came and they said what music do
huge dorks listen to? And I gave them your walkman
and they went back to space.

Lyle: Susy—

Susy: Mom has it.

Lyle: Oh.

Susy: She's listening to it in the tub.

Lyle: So, uh . . . How's she doing?

Susy: I dunno. Are you staying home tonight?

Lyle: No. I have to work.

Susy: Oh.

Lyle: What?

Susy: That leaves me here all alone.

Lyle: It'll be okay.

Susy: How do you know?

Lyle: Just . . . stay out of her way.

Susy: Like I get in her way. Like I'm saying, "Oh there's her way, I think I'll get in it." You think you're out of her way and then the way changes before you notice, and then there you are. In her way.

Lyle: Just play in your room and go to bed early. Keep your door closed.

Susy: She didn't use to be this way.

Lyle: She's worse now.

Susy: Why?

Lyle: . . . She drinks too much potion.

Susy: Too much potion?

Lyle: Way too much.

Susy: Oh.

Lyle: I gotta go.

Lyle tries to go.

Susy: Lyle. Am I a terrible little girl?

Lyle: What? No.

Susy: Mom says I made Dad go away.

Lyle: Oh man.

Susy: Is it true, Lyle? Did I make Dad go away?

Lyle: No. Mom made Dad go away.

Susy: How?

Lyle: By saying stuff like that.

Susy: I'm not a terrible little girl?

Lyle: No way. You're the best.

Susy: The best?

Lyle: The best ever.

Susy: Mom doesn't think so.

Lyle: Hey. What're you?

Susy: I'm rubber.

Lyle: What's Mom?

Susy: She's glue.

Lyle: Who's your big brother?

Susy: You are.

Lyle: And who's not gonna let anything bad happen?

Susy: You are.

Lyle: Who's the Kling Klang King?

Susy: You're the Kling Klang King of the Rim Ram Room.

Lyle: Yes I am. So you don't have anything to worry about, okay?

Susy: Okay.

Lyle: Okay. I gotta go.

Susy: Okay.

Lyle: Okay.

Lyle tries to go.

Susy: Do you want to hear a joke?

Lyle: I gotta go Susy.

Susy: How do you catch an elephant?

Lyle: I'm gonna be late.

Susy: How do you catch an elephant?

Lyle: Susy. I want to hear the joke, but I have to go now.

Susy: You have to?

Lyle: Yes. Play in your room and go to bed early.

Susy: She just comes in anyhow.

Lyle: Then lock your door if you want.

Susy: You don't want to know how to catch an elephant?

Lyle: Night Susy.

Exit.

Susy: G'night.

Pause.

Susy is terrified to be alone. She tells the joke to herself to calm down while she drags a chair over to block her bedroom door. She is in tears by the end.

Susy: How do you catch an elephant? I don't know Susy, how do you catch an elephant? Well, I'll tell you. First, you dig a big hole. And you fill up the hole with ashes. Then, all around the edge of the hole you put peas. Then, when the elephant comes up to take a pea, you kick him in the ash hole . . . You kick him in the ash-hole.

She slumps to the ground by her chair. Pause. There is a knock at her door. Susy jumps. Sharon, her Mom, talks to her through the door. She's holding a tumbler of booze.

Sharon: Hey Susy, you in there? Susy? SUSY? Are you in there?

Susy: . . . Yes.

Sharon: How you doing, kid?

Susy: Fine.

Sharon: Good. . . . Um, what did you have for lunch today?

Susy: What did I have for lunch today?

Sharon: Yeah. I uh, I wasn't feeling good this morning so I slept in, and uh, I never made you lunch.

Susy: Lyle gave me some money.

Sharon: Oh.

Susy: I bought lunch at the Mac's.

Sharon: For Christ's sake Susy, that's not good for you.

Susy: I'm sorry.

Sharon: You'll get all fat eating that crap.

Pause.

Sharon: Anyhow . . . I wanted to say that I was sorry.
About not making your lunch. I wasn't feeling good.
I had to miss work, even. I was really sick.

Pause.

Sharon: Susy?

Pause.

Sharon: Your door's locked, Susy.

Susy: Yeah, I'm—uh.

Sharon: Your door's locked.

Susy gets up and moves away from the door. She doesn't move the chair. She stands defensively and waits.

Sharon: Susy?

Susy: I'm dressing.

Sharon: I'm your mother.

Susy: I'm getting dressed.

Sharon: Open this door Susy.

Pause.

Sharon: SUSY!?

Pause.

Sharon: I don't like locked doors in my house, Susy!

Pause.

Sharon: OPEN THIS DOOR!!

Susy: . . . No.

Sharon: What did you say? I am your mother. Did you say no to me? I am your mother and you will open this door right now or I'll break the friggin' thing down. OPEN THIS DOOR!

Pause.

Sharon: OPEN THIS GODDAMN DOOR!

Pause.

Sharon: *Becoming calmly cruel.* This is terrible behaviour for a young girl, Susy. This is . . . disgraceful behaviour and it just shows what kind of little girl you're turning out to be. It just shows that you're a terrible little girl. It's no wonder your father left.

Pause.

Sharon: No one loves a terrible little girl, Susy! Do you hear me? DO YOU HEAR ME? OPEN THIS DOOR! . . . Open this door . . .

Pause.

Sharon: Oh. Oh God.

Sharon walks away from the door. Susy listens. Susy decides to check.

Susy: Mom? Just a minute, okay, I just have to—

Susy moves the chair and opens the door. Nobody is there.

Susy: Mom?

THE TEENS

Two: How was the exam?

One: Had better.

Three: How gross is that?

Two: What happened?

One: Math was never my strong suit. And my Dad says that I know the math, I just don't have confidence that I know it.

Two: Your Dad said that?

Three: What a weirdo.

One: And what gives you more confidence than a couple of drinks?

Three: A couple of drinks?

One: A mickey of spiced rum.

Two: That's a lot of confidence.

Three: I studied really really hard for that exam. Even the trig which makes my head explode and the binomials and the hypotenuse and all that crap. I stayed up all night, and I drank some coffee which has always made my tummy feel funny.

Four : Pick up your pencils and begin . . . NOW!

One: All the numbers started to look funny. They started to kinda swirl.

Two: As a custodian of a school I expect to clean up a certain amount of vomit. But this was ridiculous.

One: I blew chunks right there in the exam. I covered my desk.

Three: How gross it that?

Two: I smelt it and I just couldn't help myself. I totally puked.

Three: There was puke everywhere. What could I do. I puked.

Four: And then I vomited. Right in front of the students.

One: *As someone new.* That was when I puked.

Two: *As someone new.* Me too.

Three: Everybody puked, except Sally, who's bulimic, so she pukes all the time and it doesn't matter that much.

One: I totally blew that exam. I was so upset that I skipped the afternoon and got drunk.

Two: You got drunk again that same day?

One: Yeah. So?

Two: You are totally an alcoholic.

One: I am not.

Three: How gross is that?

One: I just drink when I need confidence.

AT SHARON'S BAR

Sharon: And her door was locked. Like I was the goddamn boogie man or something. She's afraid of me. Her own mother. How do you figure that?

Bartender: I'm scared of spiders.

Sharon: It's the divorce. It screws up everybody. Them. Me.

The only happy one is him. Him and that . . . child he ran off with. That's how it is, I guess. We women get traded in and you men just get better looking. He said he was leaving 'cause I was a drunk. But I guess he didn't mind a drunk raising his kids, did he?

Bartender: I guess not.

Sharon: A lousy drunk, he said. Said it in front of Lyle, too. Just to humiliate me. But he didn't leave because I enjoy a cocktail. He left for that bimbo. That . . . Bar-ba-ra. And now I enjoy a cocktail even more. And here's the kicker. I only started drinking because Bill likes tennis!

Bartender: Come again?

Sharon: I hurt my ankle playing tennis. Tylenol threes do nothing so I switched to bourbon. I switched to bourbon, he switched to Bar-ba-ra. I think it was her little white skirt.

Bartender: Tennis is okay.

Sharon: Tennis ruined my life! Pretty soon him and Barbara were playing every day. He looked so *bewildered, hurt . . .* happy . . . *regaining her bluster.* I tell ya—this family has gone from quasi-functional to screwed-right-up in the three years since Bill left. And he doesn't know a damn thing about it.

Bartender: Would you care for another?

Pause.

Sharon: Do I drink a lot?

Bartender: It's none of my business.

Sharon: But I mean, you see people all the time, it's your job. Do you think that I drink a lot?

Bartender: It's none of my business.

Sharon: Right.

Bartender: . . . So you want that drink?

Sharon: Yes. Yes I do.

Bartender: Okay.

Sharon: So what does that make me?

Bartender: It's none of my business.

Sharon: A drinker. A lady who likes a drink or two. After a hard day's work. I work hard. Work hard, play hard.

Bartender: It's none of my business.

Sharon: It's nobody's business. I do what I want.

Bartender: Fine. The usual?

Sharon: Just one more.

Bartender: Uh huh.

Sharon: I mean it. After this, cut me off.

Bartender: I don't cut people off.

Sharon: You don't?

Bartender: Have you ever seen a drunk that's been cut off? You can't help them.

Sharon: Good point.

Bartender: It's easier to let them drink themselves into unconsciousness. Then I call them cabs and their problems remain their own. It's none of my business.

Pause.

Sharon: You're a bartender.

Bartender: Yes. Yes I am.

Sharon: You're supposed to be understanding and comforting and a good listener and that.

Bartender: I am an excellent listener. I am incredibly understanding and I have huge wellsprings of compassion and perception. I simply prefer not to use those skills at work. Because then I would be a "wise bartender," as portrayed on TV. And we are not on TV.

Sharon: Well, I hate to ask it, but I've had a hell of a night, and I need a wise and friendly bartender.

Bartender: As portrayed on TV.

Sharon: Well . . . yeah.

Bartender: You're having a tough time?

Sharon: The toughest.

Bartender: Well alright, but if I'm gonna be a TV bartender, I better get the whole TV deal.

Sharon: Like what?

Bartender: Well, for instance, TV bartenders are always having provocative conversations with beautiful women.

Sharon: . . . How beautiful do you need?

THE TEENS

One: Let me begin by saying, I was totally pissed.

Two: Wasted?

Three: Pissed.

Four: How pissed?

One: Wrecked. On account of having shotgun six beers standing in the bathtub with my man Chauncy who really shouldn't've been driving.

Two: But we went the back way.

Four: We drove real slow.

Three: Hardly any traffic.

Two: We gotta get to the party.

One: Totally pissed. But Chauncy swears it just makes him a better driver and I was too drunk to argue.

Two: So Eddy's cousin from the city came up with like twenty tabs of acid. He's selling 'em for ten bucks a pop, even though I know where he comes from they go for five.

Four: What a dink—

Two: But on the other hand, hey, acid!

One: So we're on the road, swerving a bit, it's true. And we see this car coming the other way, so Chauncy's really pissed, so he thinks it'll be totally funny to flash his lights on and off and play La Cukaroacha on the horn.

Two: And we are just trippin' in the back seat.

Four: Okay, everyone can stop growing horns anytime now!

Three: My hand is a pumpkin, then it's a fish, then it's my hand again.

Two: And the car comin' down the road. It's a cop car.

Four: Step out of the car, please.

Two: But we are trippin' so hard . . .

Four: The cop is an alien. THE COP IS AN ALIEN!

Two: That Jones figures it's a good idea to go for the cop's gun.

One: The cop just elbows him in the head. Jones goes down. And the cop starts persecuting with extreme prejudice.

Two: Pretty soon it's all billy clubs and handcuffs and Chauncy is getting the breathalyzer. Four more cop cars show up.

One: Jones won't stop singing.

Four: SOMEWHERE! OVER THE RAINBOW!

Three: Chauncy loses his license. I think forever. I think even when Chauncy grows up and has kids, his kids lose their license.

One: And we all have to pick up garbage at the skating rink for our community hours.

Two: And my parents think I'm a criminal. Just because I got convicted of a crime.

Three: One hundred hours. That's like four months of weekends.

Four: Except for Eddy's cousin, who got caught with all that acid, which is called trafficking. He got tried as an adult and now is in prison and has a large boyfriend.

Three: And you missed the party!

One: How was it?

Two: Good party.

Three: Fine party.

Four: Great party.

MORNING, THE KITCHEN

Lyle is pouring a bottle down the sink. Susy enters with the bartender.

Susy: Look Lyle! Mommy had a sleepover!

Lyle: Step away from the strange man, Susy. Eat your cereal.

Bartender: Uh, hello.

Lyle: Hello. You must be a friend of our dear mother. I'm Lyle and you've met Susy. What might your name be?

Bartender: I'm the bartender.

Lyle: I see. So that makes you less a friend of my mother, than a kind of professional associate.

Bartender: What?

Lyle: It doesn't matter. I haven't made coffee because it stunts our growth, but I guess you'd like some, huh?

Bartender: Yeah. If it's—

Lyle: No trouble at all. Any one-night stand my drunken mother brings home deserves all the compassion I can muster.

Bartender: Your brother talks pretty fast.

Susy: *Smiles.* Yeah.

Lyle: I'll thank you not to address my sister. She's young yet, you see, and I'd like her to stay that way for the natural amount of time.

Bartender: I'm sorry—I didn't mean anything.

Lyle: No. I'm sure you don't mean anything at all.

Sharon enters.

Sharon: Morning, sweety.

Susy: Hi.

Lyle: Susy. Here's your lunch. You have to catch your bus.

Susy: Nice to meet you.

Bartender: Bye.

Sharon: Have a good day, sweety.

Susy: Is he going to be our new Dad?

Lyle: Go to the bus stop Susy, I'll be there soon.

Susy exits.

Lyle: Well, I'm sure you two have a lot to discuss. You'll probably want to find out each other's names and—

Sharon: Please, Lyle. I have a headache.

Lyle: What a surprise! I think I might faint dead away from the weight of that shock.

Sharon: *Opens the cupboard.* Lyle—

Lyle: What?

Sharon: . . . I am the parent here, Lyle.

Lyle: Really?

Sharon: Yes. So watch your tongue.

Pause.

Lyle: Where do I work?

Sharon: Here we go.

Lyle: You're the parent. You must have some working knowledge of your children's lives. Where do I work?

Sharon: Lyle, where is—

Lyle: No, you're right. That's a tough one. How about this? How's Susy doing at school?

Sharon: Lyle, stop this.

Lyle: Another tough one. You're right, I'm being unfair. This one is so easy, even you will get it. What grade am I in? What grade am I in, Mother?

Sharon: Eleven.

Lyle: Give the lady a prize. I guess you're the prize, huh, what was your name again?

Bartender: I'm the bartender.

Lyle: You're the bartender. Good. Let's all call each other by our titles. You're the bartender. I'm the child. You say you're the parent. Right? That's what you say?

Sharon: Lyle, you are—

Lyle: Embarrassing you? In front of your bartender. What a terrible child I must be.

Sharon: Yes.

Lyle: Yes. You're right. I'm not at all suited to my position. In fact I may be leaving the organization completely. Then you wouldn't have to bother with struggling to be the parent. You could just follow your calling, and be a drunk.

Sharon: Where is it, Lyle?

Lyle: You didn't hear a word I said, did you?

Sharon: Where is it?

Lyle: . . . You make me sick.

Lyle exits.

Sharon: I don't know what to say.

Bartender: It must be very hard to have a kid that talks so
fast.

Sharon: It is this morning.

Bartender: He seems very angry with you.

Pause.

Sharon: Look, you have to go.

Bartender: I do?

Sharon: I have to be a different kind of—I can't be—Just
go, okay.

Bartender: Perhaps I could help—

Sharon: Get out.

Bartender: Alright.

Pause.

Bartender: I had a nice time.

Sharon: Great. Bye.

Bartender: Bye.

Sharon sits at the table with her head in her hands.

TEEN SCENE

One: Ever had your stomach pumped? The only good

thing about it is that you're usually unconscious when it happens.

Two: The game is called ten in ten. Ten beers in ten minutes. It separates the men from the boys.

Three: Right around graduation is the busy time for us paramedics. We pump a lotta stomachs. We got a bet going. Last year it was what?

Four: Twenty-eight stomachs.

Three: And the year before?

Four: Twenty-four stomachs.

Three: I say we break thirty this year.

Four: I say we don't.

Three: We bet ten bucks.

Four: And—

Three: And the loser has to get his stomach pumped.

One: I don't remember much. But apparently I stood up in the middle of the room, projectile vomited on the television, punched my best friend and started doing the funky chicken naked on the pool table. Normally I'm a very shy person.

Two: Chicks rarely complete the ten in ten. I was gonna ask her to grad, until I saw the puke on my TV. I couldn't be all that mad, though. Because Denise was obviously very messed up.

One: I have a dim memory of feeling incredibly cold. And I tried to get a blanket, but I already had everybody's coats on me. And I was still freezing. But then everything went black.

Three: But sometimes people don't call in time to get their stomach pumped, and that's bad news.

Four: You could die.

Three: It's bad.

Four: It completely sucks.

A beeper goes off.

Three: Ah! Get out the stomach pump!

Four: Damn.

Three: I'm gonna win!

Four: You are not.

AT THE HOUSE

Lyle and Buddy doing homework. Susy plays nearby.

Buddy: *Putting down a book.* Wow. Holy cow, man. I don't believe it.

Lyle: What.

Buddy: Mr. Hyde.

Lyle: Yeah?

Buddy: He was Dr. Jekyll the whole time.

Lyle: You didn't know that?

Susy: What are you reading?

Buddy: An excellent book. *The Strange Case of Dr. Jekyll and Mr. Hyde.* And get this, they're the same guy!

Susy: What are you talking about?

Buddy: Okay, there's this guy, a doctor guy, sweet lovely guy, right? And there's this other guy. This mean horrible monster of a guy, who does terrible nasty stuff. But it turns out they're the same guy!

Susy: They're the same guy?

Buddy: Yeah, cause the sweet lovely doctor invented this potion and he drank too much of it, and it turned him into the monster guy.

Lyle: I can't believe the level of your surprise.

Susy: Waitaminute. He drank too much potion?

Buddy: Yeah.

Susy: And it made him mean?

Buddy: Yeah. Changed him into a whole different guy.

Susy: Just like Mom.

Buddy: Oops.

Susy: Just like what happens with Mom. Right?

Lyle: Well—

Susy: She drinks too much potion. You said so.

Lyle: It's a little bit like that.

Susy: What's different?

Lyle: Well when Dr. Jekyll turned into Mr. Hyde his whole appearance changed.

Susy: So does Mom's! Her eyes get puffy and her hair gets messy, and—

Lyle: Dr. Jekyll's potion was a bit like Mom's, but his was stronger.

Susy: He had a stronger potion?

Lyle: Yeah.

Susy: Oh.

Lyle: Let me be more clear—

Buddy: *Looking out a window.* Dude, your Mom's home.

Lyle: It's Friday, Buddy. Friday is bar night.

Buddy: Well maybe it's house party night.

Lyle: Buddy. You gotta go.

Buddy: I'd like to meet her just once.

Lyle: You will never meet her. Please, go.

Buddy: Okay. Just let me get my coat. *He gets his coat really slowly.*

Lyle: Hurry up, man.

Buddy: I'm . . . goin' . . . as . . . fast . . . as I can.

Susy: *At the window.* She has groceries.

Lyle: She bought groceries?

Sharon: Hello.

Lyle: Hello mother. We didn't expect you home.

Sharon: Well, I'm home. I'm home and I've bought groceries and I rented a movie for me and Susy. Are you going out?

Lyle: I don't know.

Sharon: If you're staying in, I could go get a more grown-up movie for us. I rented *Flubber*. Have you seen it, Susy?

Susy: Yes.

Sharon: Oh.

Susy: But I wanna see it again.

Sharon: Great . . . So who's your friend?

Lyle: This is Buddy.

Buddy: Pleased to make your acquaintance Mrs. Bundaberg.

Sharon: The pleasure's mine, Buddy. Would you like to stay for supper?

Lyle: Buddy's gotta go.

Buddy: No I don't.

Lyle: He was just leaving.

Sharon: Another time. . . . Well, I'm going to start on dinner.

Exit.

Buddy: Dude, your Mom's totally nice.

Lyle: Buddy, you don't know anything.

Buddy: Can I stay for dinner?

Lyle: It's out of the question.

Buddy: Dude, my Dad can't cook at all.

Lyle: Buddy, get out of here.

Buddy: Alright, man. But you're being very impolite.

Exit.

Susy: What's wrong with you?

Lyle: Nothing.

Susy: Mom's being nice.

Lyle: Are you gonna fall for that? That is not what she's like.

Susy: That's what she's like without potion.

Lyle: What?

Susy: When she doesn't have her potion she's nice, and when she does she's mean. Just like in the book.

Lyle: What book?

Susy: Buddy's book. With the nice doctor and the mean guy. Exactly like the book.

Lyle: No. . . . No. Not like in the book. This is real life, Susy. This is not some book.

Susy: It seems just like the book to me.

Lyle: Look Susy, Mom may seem all nice right now, but if she gets through tonight without . . . drinking her potion, I'll—

Susy: But she's being nice.

Lyle: Susy, I—Dammit!

Susy: Why are you so mad?

Lyle: Because—

Susy: She's being nice.

Lyle: I know. Just when I'm getting everything arranged, she has to . . . be nice.

Susy: You don't want her to be nice?

Lyle: Of course . . . I do.

Susy: What are you getting all arranged?

Pause.

Lyle: Would you like to live someplace else?

Susy: What?

Lyle: Away from Mom, where she would never get all drunk and yell or anything.

Susy: Whaddaya mean?

Lyle: I mean our own place. An apartment of our own.

Susy: Well, if she stays nice I wanna stay here.

Lyle: It won't last, Susy. It can't. She can't help it.

Susy: She's making dinner.

Lyle: I know—

Susy: She rented *Flubber*.

Lyle: I KNOW—

Susy: Don't yell.

Lyle: I'm sorry, Susy.

Susy: Besides, maybe there's an antidote.

Lyle: What?

Susy: To the potion.

Lyle: No, Susy—there's—

Sharon: The sauce is on. Come and taste it and let me know what it needs, okay?

Susy: Okay, Mommy. *Running into the kitchen.*

Lyle: So you made dinner.

Sharon: Yep.

Lyle: And that makes everything okay?

Sharon: I'm not sure the sauce is quite that good.

Pause.

You could give me a break, you know.

Lyle: No. I couldn't.

Exits.

THE TEENS

One: It would've been fine, except I was so drunk.

Two: Wasted?

One: Pissed.

Two: How pissed?

One: Wrecked. So I get home, and I'm heading right to my room, cause I'm getting the spins and I gotta lie down and look at my lamp.

Two: It's the only thing that helps.

One: Right. Except my Dad is totally pissed too and it turns out, he just smoked his last cigarette.

Two: Oh man.

Three: *A young boy talking to his grandma as she drives.* Grandma, you don't know anything. Batman could totally beat up Goldberg.

Four: *As Grandma.* I'm just not so sure.

Three: Gram! Batman has training far beyond any wrestler, plus the full use of his amazing utility belt.

Four: I still think Mr. Goldberg would have a good chance.

One: And my Dad. He'll think nothing of going out drunk and shooting at sparrows with his ten gauge. But he won't drive. Even one beer and he won't drive. He just won't. Something that happened in high school or something.

Two: What about your Mom?

One: It's a family affair, man. Mom's throwing up downstairs, she's out of the game. That leaves me to drive Dad to the store. He needs his cigarettes.

Two: But you're wasted.

One: Right.

Two: Did you come clean?

One: Not a chance.

Three: And also don't forget that Batman is avenging his parents, okay? He's motivated. Goldberg just does it for the money.

One: So, I'm on the road, Dad's got his head out the window, it's dark out, and what's more, it's raining.

Two: Worst possible situation.

Three: Also, Batman has Robin to back him up and if he's in big trouble, Superman'll come. You don't think Goldberg could beat up Superman, do you?

Four: I don't know. That Goldberg—

Three: GRAMMA!

One: It was raining.

Three: Superman isn't even human!

One: It was dark.

Three: He is completely invulnerable!

One: I should not have been driving.

Three: His heat vision alone!

One: I should not have been driving.

Three: Gramma, watch out!

Pause.

Two: And that's why everybody's dead.

Three: We are gathered here today . . .

One: I'm sorry.

Two: And you're dead too.

Three: To remember a family.

One: I'm so sorry.

Two: It's too late.

One: How late?

Two: Really late.

LYLE AND BUDDY

Buddy is rolling a joint.

Buddy: The thing that most people don't realize is that alcohol is a drug. It's a depressant, it dehydrates one terribly. It's quite addictive and leads to liver disease, domestic violence, and a staggering number of traffic fatalities. But people underestimate its physical and societal detriment. And why? Because it's legal. Whereas marijuana—*He smokes a bit. Pause.*

Lyle: Yeah?

Buddy: It's more . . . softer . . . like a bunny will hop on a field . . . just hop hop hop and it doesn't . . . grrrrr . . . you know make you all mad . . . or . . . nothing . . . and wheee, it's so . . . just . . . I'm sorry, what was the question?

Pause.

Lyle: We've been friends since we were kids, right Buddy?

Buddy: Dude.

Lyle: And our friendship has lasted despite of many things that can break a friendship up.

Buddy: I know, man.

Lyle: Like the fact that you're two grades behind me, even though we're the same age.

Buddy: *Toking.* School is tough, man.

Lyle: And the fact that you often fall asleep when I'm talking to you.

Buddy: Dude, I'm sorry about that. But you talk so fast sometimes man, and I get tired.

Lyle: What's my phone number?

Buddy: I hate it when you do this man—

Lyle: Just humour me.

Buddy: Okay I don't remember.

Lyle: Buddy—

Buddy: But I don't need to remember, cause I wrote it down on this piece of paper I keep in my pocket.

Lyle: Buddy, I've had the same phone number since we were six. Why can't you remember?

Buddy: *Toking.* I forget things.

Lyle: Did you ever think that maybe pot makes you dumb? . . . Buddy?

Buddy: I'm sorry. I was looking at my thumb.

Lyle: Forget it.

Buddy: No problem. Oh. That reminds me. We got a letter.

Lyle: A letter, or *the* letter?

Buddy: A letter?

Lyle: From "Moms against Teen Drinking"?

Buddy: Yeah, I think.

Lyle: Why didn't you say so before?

Buddy: *Toking.* I forgot.

Lyle: *Ripping it open.* Oh boy.

Buddy: We regret to inform you that we received so many excellent entries—

Lyle: No Buddy. No. We won man. We won the contest.

Buddy: No way!

Lyle: Way.

Buddy: No way!

Lyle: Look!

Buddy: Hot damn. Five grand, baby!

Lyle: Five grand.

Buddy: We split it right down the middle.

Lyle: Um—

Buddy: That's like—three grand each! Right on!

Lyle: Buddy. How would you feel if we didn't share the money in a completely equal fashion?

Pause.

Buddy: Talk slow.

Lyle: I'm talking slow.

Buddy: Don't talk fast on me.

Lyle: I'm not. I just—me and Susy. We need our own place. Cause my Mom is—And if we could keep a little more of the money, it would help a lot.

Buddy: You're serious about that.

Lyle: Dead serious.

Buddy: I don't know any high school guys with their own pad, man.

Lyle: I'm a pioneer, Buddy. I'm breaking new ground.

Buddy: Why do you need your own place?

Lyle: Why? We—me and Susy, we—we need it.

Buddy: How come?

Lyle: We just do, okay.

Buddy: Tell me why, and you can have it all.

Lyle: Well. My Mom—

Buddy: Yeah—

Lyle: *Breaking down a bit.* She's uh—

Buddy: Uh huh?

Lyle: She's an alchoholic.

Buddy hugs him.

Buddy: Attaboy.

THE TEENS

One: For my science project this year, I have decided to tackle this problem, which has plagued humanity for generations. Can a person host a party without having to clean up vomit? Thank you for participating in our experiment.

Two: Five beers. One bottle of water. Three bags of chips.

Three: *Sadly.* One designated driver.

One: I thank you for your sacrifice.

Three: Shut up.

One: I understand.

Four: One basement with no breakable items inside.

One: We found that forty-six per cent of vomiting can be traced to mixing different types of hard alcohol together in slurpees. This was found to also be the leading cause of being busted for raiding your parent's liquor cabinet.

Four: Another thirty per cent of vomiting was traced to drinking beers numbered six through eleven. Coolers can cause vomiting almost immediately. Tequila has been linked not only to vomiting, but to waking up in foreign countries, with no pants.

Three: We also found that ninety-two per cent of drunk driving is caused by the driver being drunk.

One: Thanks again, man.

Three: Shut up.

One: By limiting the alcohol to beer, and limiting the beers to five, I had absolutely no vomit to clean up.

Two: I puked at home the next morning.

One: I don't care about that.

SUSY AND SHARON AT HOME

Sharon: How was your spaghetti?

Susy: Good.

Sharon: Good. I was never much of a cook. That was more your father's thing. He cooked and I did the dishes. Now I cook and do the dishes.

Susy: Lyle cooks pretty good.

Sharon: Your brother takes good care of you doesn't he?

Susy: Yeah.

Sharon: He just will not give me a break. I mean here I am, trying so hard.

Susy: The spaghetti was good.

Sharon: I want a drink so bad, Susy.

Susy: I'll get some milk.

Sharon: That's not what I want to drink.

Susy: You want some potion.

Sharon: Potion?

Susy: That what Lyle said it was.

Sharon: God he hates me.

Susy: No.

Sharon: He hates my guts.

Susy: He's just mad at you. For drinking potion.

Sharon: I'm gonna have just a little drink right now. Okay? Just to show you that it's nothing evil or anything.

Susy: Really?

Sharon: Just to show that it doesn't bubble or hiss or make me a monster.

Susy: Do you have to?

Sharon: You know Susy. I think I do.

Susy: . . . Can I be excused to go play in my room?

Pause.

Sharon: Sure. You're excused. All my children are excused. I'll be right here.

Susy: Don't drink too much potion, okay. If you can help it.

Sharon: God, what do you think I am?

Susy: Please?

Pause.

AT A BUS STOP

Lyle waits. The bartender is there.

Bartender: Hello.

Lyle: Oh. Hi.

Bartender: I'm the bartender. From the other morning.

Murray Utas as the Bartender, and Chris Bullough as Lyle.
PHOTO BY SOPHIE LEES.

Lyle: I remember. . . . Now that we're alone at a dark bus stop, I—uh—I certainly hope there aren't any hard feelings.

Bartender: No. You're angry with your mother. It's none of my business.

Lyle: Cool.

Pause.

Bartender: . . . So. You're planning to leave home.

Lyle: Excuse me?

Bartender: You're unsuited to your position. You're . . . leaving the organization.

Lyle: You have quite a memory.

Bartender: I'm a good listener, on my own time.

Lyle: Yeah.

Bartender: Your mother seems bent on reformation.

Lyle: And how do you know that?

Bartender: She kicked me out right after your little talk. She wasn't at the bar tonight and she always is. Sounds like an attempt to me.

Lyle: Listen, Mr. Bartender. A drunken fling with my mother does not entitle you to advise on our personal matters.

Bartender: It wasn't a drunken fling.

Lyle: No?

Bartender: I don't drink.

Lyle: . . . You're braver than I thought.

Bartender: I can understand that you wouldn't want me involved in your affairs, so I'll just say one more thing. Your mother's drinking, it's a disease. You can't cure it, you didn't cause it, and you can't control it.

Lyle: *Shrugs.* I know that.

Bartender: Oh, you do?

Lyle: I read it someplace.

Bartender: *A little taken aback.* Well. Good.

Pause.

Lyle: So, can I ask? Why are you a bartender, anyway? You talk like some kinda AA counsellor. Something doesn't fit.

Bartender: At the bar I make drinks. After work, I do as much good as possible.

Lyle: With little talks like this?

Bartender: Yes. *Notices the BARTENDER signal.* But I also fight crime.

Lyle: You fight crime?

Bartender: See that spotlight with the martini shaker symbol in the middle?

Lyle: Yeah.

Bartender: That's for me.

He throws off his overcoat and is dressed like a superhero beneath.

Bartender: It means the Bartender is needed.

Lyle: Wait a minute.

Bartender: I don't have a minute, Lyle. Someone is in danger! IT'S CLO-O-O-O-O-O-SING TIME!!! *He flies away.*

Lyle: Wow.

AT HOME

Susy is in the bathroom. She talks to herself as if she were a scientist and a journalist interviewing the scientist.

Susy: The problem with Mommy is the potion. That's the problem. If she had the antidote, there would be no problem, isn't that right Susy?

—It certainly is. And that is what brings us to the laboratory today.

Susy begins mixing all kinds of household products together.

You'll be given lots of scientific awards for this important discovery, Susy.

—Oh, that's not important. The important thing is that I save my mother from the evil potion.

Yes, yes of course that is the important thing.

—Of course to get her to drink the antidote, we'll have to mix it with her potion. It's all she'll drink when she's in this state.

She pours some scotch into her brew.

Sharon: Susy?

Susy: Yes of course, very clever.

Sharon: SUSY?

Susy: Yes?

Sharon: Did you fall in?

Susy: *Putting away all the household items.* No. I was just making you a drink. *Susy opens the door.*

Sharon: Oh. Well, that is very civilized of you, Susy. Thank you.

Susy: You're welcome.

Sharon: It's nice to have a little co-operation around here.

Susy: *Grabbing her soda.* Mommy, you know what would be fun?

Sharon: What, honey?

Susy: A chugalug contest.

Sharon: Wha—

Susy: I bet I can drink my drink before you can drink yours.

Sharon: I've had a lot of practice, honey.

Susy: I'll make your bed all week if you win.

Sharon: Really?

Susy: Sure.

Sharon: Well, alright, you're on.

Susy: Okay, go.

They drink their drinks as fast as they can. Susy stops drinking first to look at how her Mom is taking it.

Sharon: *Finishing.* Jesus. Susy. What was in that?

Susy: It was the antidote! Now you're all better!

Sharon pauses. Then drops to the floor. Long pause.

Beth Graham as Susy and Chris Bullough as Lyle.
PHOTO BY MIKE REICHERT STEINHAUER.

Susy: Mommy?

Lyle enters.

Susy: Oh Mommy? Mommy?

Lyle: Oh Jesus. What the hell is this?

Susy: *Really upset.* She drank the . . . and she . . . I was just—

Lyle: It's okay Susy. It's not your fault.

Susy: IT IS, THOUGH, IT—

Lyle: Jesus. Dammit, oh Jesus. I have to call an ambulance. Oh man.

Susy: It's my fault.

Lyle: Stay here with Mom, I have to call an ambulance.

Susy: I'm sorry Mommy.

Lyle: Oh Jesus.

Susy: I'm sorry.

Lyle: Hello, I need an ambulance to 112 Elm Street.

Susy: I was trying to fix you.

Lyle: It's my mother. It looks like alcohol poisoning.

Susy: I was trying . . .

Lyle: Well, that's cause she's—she's an alcoholic.

Susy: I was trying to make it all better.

Lyle: Thank you. *Hangs up.*

Susy: I'm sorry.

Lyle: The ambulance is coming, Susy. Is she breathing?

Susy: Yes.

Lyle: The ambulance is coming.

Susy: It's my fault, Lyle.

Lyle: Listen Susy. This is not your fault.

Susy: No, Lyle. It's my fault.

Lyle: It's not your fault Susy. It's very important that you realize that.

Susy: . . . Are you sure?

Lyle: I am positive.

Susy: . . . Okay.

Lyle: Do you see now Susy? We have to go away from here. She can't take care of herself, let alone us. We have to take care of each other. It's just you and me, okay, Susy. Okay?

Susy: But, Lyle, I—

Lyle: You and me, Susy. Okay?

Susy: Okay.

Lyle: Okay.

LYLE'S LETTER

Lyle: Dear Mom. I guess if you're reading this, you're conscious now. That's good. I hope you stay that way. Susy told me how she accidentally poisoned you trying to make you an antidote. It's sort of my fault, cause I told her you drank potion, instead of scotch. She feels really bad so I told her it was okay. I hope that it's okay. You've probably noticed that Susy and me moved out. We found a little place that I can afford. A least for a while. We didn't do it to make you feel bad or punish you or anything. We just needed to get away. I'm not gonna tell you where we are right now, but I hope you won't try to find us. At least not until you get a little better. And please don't tell social services on us, because then we'd get separated and put in foster homes and that would defeat the purpose of everything. Just trust that I can take care of us for a while. I hope that you can take care of yourself. Love Lyle.

The scene shifts to Sharon at her AA meeting. She is reading the letter out loud to the meeting. The bartender is there.

Sharon: *Overlapping with Lyle.* Just trust that I can take care of us for a while. I hope that you can take care of yourself. Love Lyle. Lyle. He's my oldest son. He wrote me this letter. Well, it's all in the letter. I, uh— have another child—a daughter, named Susy and uh—Lyle made this commercial, for a contest—

One: I've seen that commercial.

Two: Good commercial.

One: Fine commercial.

Sharon: Great commercial, but it uh—um—it made me see that—oh—

Bartender: Tell them your name.

Sharon: Right. And uh—I'm Sharon—

The Meeting: Hi Sharon.

Sharon: Hi. Um. Hi everyone. Uh—

Bartender: It's okay.

Sharon: My name is Sharon and—I'm an alcoholic.

SUSY

Susy: In the movie I saw? About the snowy little town that was afraid of the avalanche? Here's how it ends. In the town there's this guy. This young guy who's tired of being afraid of the snow all the time. So he goes to the middle of town and he screams as loud as he can, waiting for the snow to come and bury him. And some snow comes down, but not an avalanche. Just a little snow and they shovel it away and it's okay. It's better than okay, in fact, because the people in the town get to make some noise when they want to now. They're not scared all the time. They're free.

Do It Right

by Chris Craddock

directed by Sophie Lees

THEATRE PRODUCTION
spring tour 2001

Do It Right

Production History

Do It Right was workshopped under the direction of Sophie Lees by Azimuth Theatre in December 2000.

Cast

Joey's Dad / Father Michael / Ben / Leo / Brad
Chris Bullough
Leo's Dad / Joey / Daryll *Michael Scholar Jr.*
Becky's Mom / Jen *Twilla MacLeod*
Jen's Mom / Becky / Laverne *Annie Dugan*

Do It Right was first produced under the direction of Sophie Lees by Azimuth Theatre in April 2001.

Cast

Becky's Mom / Jen *Juliann Wilding*
Leo's Dad / Daryll / Joey / Ben *Chris Postle*
Joey's Dad / Leo / Brad / Father Michael
Collin Doyle
Becky / Jen's Mom / Laverne *Twilla MacLeod*

Designer *Marissa Kochanski*
Costumes *Warren Pullen*
Sound Design *Jose Teodoro*
Stage / Road manager *Keri Strobel*

The Characters
Jen—sixteen, good-hearted girl
Becky—sixteen, good-hearted, with an edge
Daryll—sixteen, basically sweet and clueless
Brad—sixteen, gay
Leo—ten, impressionable
Joey—ten, Leo's leader
Laverne—crusty, nineteen, no nonsense type
Ben—three
Father Michael—forty-five, compassionate, religious
Leo's Dad
Becky's Mom
Joey's Dad
Jen's Mom

Production Notes
The Azimuth Theatre production was done with four actors in multiple castings. The play could be done with more actors, but not less. The premiere production used a series of signs—sometimes titling scenes, sometimes in a thought bubble to denote characters' inner workings—but slides would be equally effective. Feel free to add local references wherever appropriate and to update any references to elements of popular culture.

Sign: WHAT OUR PARENTS TOLD US

Sign: LEO AND HIS DAD

Leo's Dad: *With a diagram.* This is the average honey bee. The honey bee travels from flower to flower in search of nectar, which it collects from the male parts of the flower, if you will accept the term. The nectar mixes with the bee's saliva and is regurgitated in the form of honey. Accidentally in this process pollen is collected on the head and legs of the bee which is then transported to the next flower. If the pollen comes into contact with the female parts of the flower, if you will accept the term, a new flower begins to be generated. And that's how sex works.

Leo: What?

Sign: BECKY AND HER MOM

Becky's Mom: When time has passed in a relationship and a loving mutual oneness has been attained, there come certain urges to be physically pleasurable to one another. Certain mergings may exist in this blissful togetherness, and if really and truly in love you may even allow his wand to illuminate your sacred space. And that's how sex works.

Becky: His wand?

Sign: JOEY AND HIS DAD

Joey's Dad brings out a chair and a broom. He props the broom in the chair so it remains rampant and unrolls a condom onto it.

Joey's Dad: And that's all you need to know.

Joey: Where does the broom come in?

Sign: JEN AND HER MOM

Jen's Mom: Your father and I were just wrestling. Just playing, you know, just fooling around—no, not that, um—anyway, we both thought it was time to talk with you, share with you about . . . um . . .

Jen: Sex?

Jen's Mom: No. Yes. Yes, because you are getting to an age, when sex is . . . it becomes a thing to do. Not that it's a thing to do, like playing bridge, not that it's to be a chore. It should be special and nice, but also very serious, VERY VERY serious, something that you undertake with gravity and a . . . and a lawyer . . . and that's not to say that . . . if you were to meet a man, later, when you're a woman . . . Oh Jen, you're just a girl now, a kid, and this thing—and boys never . . . Sex . . . exists . . . and you should do it hardly ever, and not until you're much older. *Huge sigh of relief.* And that's how sex works.

Jen: Mom, I have a question—

Jen's Mom: What? No—I—let's not—

Jen: It might be important—

Jen's Mom: Is that your father home from work? I thought—

Jen: Mom, I think I might be—

Jen's Mom: *Covering her ears.* LA LA LA I can't hear you.

Jen: Mom, I need—

Jen's Mom: LA LA LA . . .

Jen: *Thought bubble:* Thanks a lot.

Sign: GIRL TALK

Becky and Jen are heading to Becky's room in a bit of a hurry.
Leo tries to follow them.

Leo: What are you doing?

Becky: Nothing Leo. Get lost for now, alright?

Leo: I can't get lost. I know my way around too well.

Becky: Go call Joey.

Leo: Joey's at hockey. I have no one to play with.

Becky: Go away or I'll take you to the kitchen and nail
your feet to the linoleum.

Leo: . . . Bye.

Jen: Lock the door.

Becky: Turn on the radio.

Jen: *She does.* Can anyone hear us?

Becky: No way. Are you ready?

Jen: I'm scared.

Becky: It's better to know.

Jen: You are such a good friend.

Becky: It's nothing.

Jen: I couldn't go to anyone else like this.

Becky: Hey, that's what friends are for.

Jen: Thank you.

Becky: You're welcome. I got the test.

Jen: I don't have to pee yet.

Becky: I got it covered.

Becky gives Jen a beer from her bag. Jen drinks deeply. They wait a second.

Jen: Okay.

Becky: Okay. Good luck.

Jen: Okay.

Becky: Okay.

Jen: Okay.

Becky: Jen. Go.

Jen: Okay. You're right. Okay. Here I go.

Jen goes into the bathroom. Becky waits. Jen returns.

Jen: The stick is in the cup, but it takes fifteen minutes.

Becky: Okay.

Jen: What should we do til then?

Becky: I dunno. You want to watch some TV?

Jen: Okay. Great. Okay.

Becky: Okay.

Becky turns it on. Pause. Jen fidgets.

Jen: Hey, a new maxi pad commercial.

Becky: Why do they always pour blue stuff on them?

Jen: It's the opposite of red.

Becky: Ah.

Pause.

Jen: Oh, Beck! I was gonna be a journalist.

Beth Graham as Jen and Twilla MacLeod as Becky.
PHOTO BY SOPHIE LEES.

Becky: Hey—

Jen: I was gonna write the important stories.

Becky: You're still gonna do that.

Jen: You think?

Becky: You have options, Jen.

Jen: Sure. I'll still be a journalist, right? And you'll—

Becky: I'll take the pictures. Just like we planned.

Jen: Right. My life isn't over.

Becky: No it's not.

Jen: No.

Becky: No.

Pause.

Jen: My life is over.

Becky: It is not over.

Jen: I'm not gonna do anything. I'm gonna die in this small town with this same hair and stretch marks.

Becky: Let's wait for the test. Let's not freak out yet.

Jen: Yeah, okay.

Becky: Okay?

Jen: Okay. Yeah.

Pause.

Jen: *Gesturing to the TV.* Hey I use those.

Becky: How are they?

Jen: Absorbant.

Becky: That's the name of the game.

Pause.

Jen: How long has it been?

Becky: Not fifteen minutes.

Jen: I'm gonna check anyway.

She goes into the bathroom.

Jen: *From the other room.* BECKY?

Becky: Is it blue?

Jen: It's blue. Oh my God it's blue. Oh no no no no no. Blue, it's blue. I'M PREGNANT! *Softer.* I'm pregnant, Beck.

Becky: Oh Jen.

Jen: Why? WHY ME? I did it all right.

Becky: I know.

Jen: I slept with one guy. ONE GUY! A guy I love. I made him wait like sixteen months. Why not that Lori chick, huh? She's a slut! Why isn't she pregnant?

Becky: Maybe she is.

Jen: She better be. *Smaller.* My life is over. It just disappeared. I'm not going to be anybody.

Becky: That's not true, Jen.

Jen: No?

Becky: No. You have options.

Jen: I have options.

Becky: Right. You just have to weigh them. And decide.

Jen: *Gasping through her tears.* Right. I'll just make a responsible informed decision.

Becky: You want some beer?

Jen: I can't drink beer, Becky. I'm pregnant.

Becky: Right.

Jen: Oh Beck, I drank that beer before, do you think—

Becky: I think it's fine.

Jen: But—okay. Yeah, okay.

Pause.

Jen: You still want to go to the dance tomorrow?

Becky: That's totally up to you.

Jen breaks down.

Jen: Oh Beck. What am I gonna do?

Sign: LEO AND JOEY FIGURE IT OUT: PART ONE

Leo: You found some stuff out?

Joey: I've been asking the older guys at hockey. Those guys got it all figured out.

Leo: Sixteen-year-olds know everything.

Joey: C'mon Leo. Sixteen-year-olds just know *most* things. Twenty-one-year-olds know everything.

Leo: Oh right. So, what do you got?

Joey: Near as I can tell, it works like this. You get a—you know.

Leo: I don't know anything.

Joey: You get a stiffy.

Leo: That much I know.

Joey: The girl. Her thing is sort of like the doors on a spaceship. There's like these six interlocking doorways that sort of open up, like brsssssssssh, brsssssssshhhhhh, brrrsssshhhh, until you get to the actual thing, which apparently is all colorful. Like a baboon's butt.

Leo: But with all the doors and all, I mean, how does it reach?

Joey: Well, it's got to be a coupla feet long.

Leo: Oh man.

Joey: It's okay. We're only ten. My brother had a growth spurt when he was fourteen. I figure it happens then.

Leo: I got a long way to go, Joey.

Joey: We all do, Leo. We all do.

Sign: OFF TO THE DANCE

Daryll and Brad wait in the car. Jen and Becky confer before going over there.

Becky: You sure you're up for this?

Jen: This is my last night of freedom.

Becky: Are you gonna tell Daryll?

Jen: We'll dance our asses off, then I'll tell Daryll.

Becky: Okay.

Jen: Unless I can't stand it, then I'll tell him sooner.

Becky: Whatever you want.

Jen: Okay.

Jen starts to go, Becky stops her.

Becky: Jen, you are so amazingly cool.

Jen: I don't feel cool.

Becky: And yet, you are.

Jen: *Beat.* Let's go dancing.

Daryll: Hey! You two look fantastic.

Overlapping.

> **Jen:** Thank you very much.

> **Becky:** Yeah, yeah.

Daryll: This is my cousin Brad. He's visiting from *(nearest small town)* I thought if Becky wasn't going with anybody, she could go with Brad, because, uh, well, because you guys kinda dress the same.

Overlapping.

> **Becky:** O my god.

> **Jen:** Daryll.

> **Brad:** Smooth Daryll.

Becky: Jen, tell me you had nothing to do with this.

Brad: I'll tell you I had nothing to do with it.

Becky: Nothing personal. I just don't date. Don't ask me.

Brad: I didn't ask you.

Becky: Good.

Brad: Great.

Becky: Perfect.

Daryll: I'm sorry. Bad idea. You're not going to the dance together. But we're still all going to the dance together.

Becky: Fine. I'll go with you, but I'm not with you.

Brad: Right. I'm going by myself. You're just here in the car.

Becky: Right. I'm near you, but not with you.

Brad: We're going to the dance near each other.

Becky: Right.

Brad: Good.

Becky: Great.

Brad: Perfect.

Daryll: All's well that ends well. We're still going together, right Jen?

Jen: Oh yeah.

Daryll: Good. Let's go.

Becky: Let's go.

Brad: Good.

Becky: Great.

Brad: Perfect.

Daryll: Okay.

Daryll starts the car.

Sign: AT THE DANCE

Brad: So you go to this school?

Becky: Yes I do.

Brad: That's too bad.

Becky: Oh, and your school is way better.

Brad: My school is exactly the same. So I know what I'm talking about.

Becky: Look. I can dis my school, cause I go here, but you have to keep the polite neutrality of a visitor.

Brad: I meant no disrespect.

Becky: Good.

Brad: I just notice that there's not a lot of people who look like us.

Becky: That's cause I'm the school weirdo. Every school has one. Somebody who likes art and dyes their hair and pierces something inappropriate. Here at Smallville High, I'm it.

Brad: You don't look so weird to me.

Becky: That's cause you're a weirdo too.

Brad: I guess I am.

Pause.

Brad: So how come you don't date?

Becky: What?

Brad: You don't date. Don't ask you.

Becky: I've promised myself I'd lose my virginity on the moon. I'm waiting for casual space travel.

Brad: I don't get it.

Becky: Look, I'm a monk, alright. I just don't date.

Brad: Why not?

Becky: Because . . . I'm a weirdo.

Brad: You're a weirdo.

Becky: Total weirdo.

Brad: Well, you're an attractive weirdo.

Becky: Here we go.

Brad: What?

Becky: First I'm attractive. Then do I want to dance? Then do I want some of your vodka? Then oh listen . . . it's a slow song. Then your hands are on my butt. Then you try to put your tongue down my throat. Just save it, alright. Just because we both can spell Trent Reznor doesn't mean we're made for each other. I'm made for no man. I don't date. And that's that.

Brad: I've got an idea. Why don't you get hostile?

Becky: I just want to be clear. I don't want you calling me a tease later.

Brad: Well you don't have to worry about me.

Becky: Oh, I don't? And why is that?

Brad: I don't date either.

Becky: You don't?

Brad: Never ever.

Becky: Really?

Brad: I swear on my hair gel.

Becky: Why not?

Brad: Why don't you?

Becky: It's none of your business.

Brad: Well it's none of your business either.

Becky: So you can promise me that you will not be trying to have sex with me tonight or at any time we might spend together in the future?

Brad: Pinky swear.

Becky: Pinky sworn. And may I say that you are wearing such a cool jacket.

Brad: Thank you very much. So, we can be friends, then?

Becky: I think so.

Brad: You want to dance?

Becky: Yes I do. Where's Jen?

Brad: Where's Daryll?

Becky: I guess Jen couldn't wait.

Brad: Seems a little hanky panky is afoot?

Becky: Nope. Not tonight.

Sign: IN DARYLL'S CAR

Jen and Daryll are kissing. Daryll tries to go to the next level. Jen pushes him away.

Daryll: What's the matter, Jen?

Jen: I don't feel like it.

Daryll: Please?

Jen: No.

Daryll: Pretty please?

Jen: No.

Daryll: If you loved me you would.

Jen: Daryll. Don't be a jerk.

Daryll: What is your problem?

SFX: electric guitar.

Jen: My problem is I'm pregnant. I'm pregnant. I'm pregnant, I'm pregnant, I'm pregnant. I'm PREGNANT!

Daryll: NOOOOOOOOOOOOOOOOOOOOOOOOO!!!!!!!!!!!

Daryll pulls a gun out of the glove box and shoots himself in the head.

Jen: NOOOOOOOOOOOOOOOOOOOOOOOOOOOOOO!!!!!

A bell sounds. Time backs up to the situation at the top.

Daryll: What's the matter, Jen.

Jen: I don't feel like it?

Daryll: Please?

Jen: No.

Daryll: Pretty please?

Jen: No.

Daryll: It builds up, you know. It becomes toxic. If we don't do it, I could die.

Jen: Daryll, don't be a jerk.

Daryll: What is your problem?

SFX: Baroque harpsicord.

Jen: It's time you knew. I am pregnant with your child.

Daryll: Are you quite sure?

Jen: My womb quivers with our sin.

Daryll: Then my work here is done. I've ruined another young lady, villain that I am. Now I'm off to my petit chateau in the south of France.

Jen: But I am disgraced!

Daryll: Yes. Yes you are. You stupid little girl. HA HA HA HA HA HA HA HA HA HA AH HA!

Jen: NOOOOOOOOOOOOOOOOOOOOOOOOOOOOO!!!!!

A bell sounds. Time backs up to the situation at the top.

Daryll: What's the matter, Jen?

Jen: I don't feel like it.

Daryll: Please?

Jen: No.

Daryll: Pretty please?

Jen: No.

Daryll: Did I do something wrong?

Jen: No.

Daryll: Then what?

Jen: I have to tell you something.

Daryll: It's a bad something.

Jen: Well—

Daryll: Oh man. You're dumping me, aren't you? This is great. Grad is coming up and you're dumping me.

Jen: That's not it, Daryll.

Daryll: It's not?

Jen: I'm pregnant—I think.

Daryll: You think?

Jen: I think.

Daryll: Did you go to a doctor?

Jen: I did a test.

Daryll: But did you go to a doctor?

Jen: Then I went to a doctor.

Daryll: And what did the doctor say?

Jen: That I'm pregnant.

Daryll: So you're pregnant for sure.

Jen: Yes.

Pause.

Daryll: That time it broke—

Jen: Must've been.

Daryll: Oh man.

Jen: Yeah.

Pause.

Daryll: Oh man.

Jen: Yeah.

Pause.

Daryll: So . . . what are you going to do?

Jen: You mean, what are we gonna do?

Daryll: Right. I guess—

Jen: We're in this together, right?

Daryll: Yeah, but—

Jen: But, what?

Daryll: It's in your belly, right.

Jen: So? So what?

Daryll: So I can't tell you what to do. It's your body.

Jen: I know that.

Daryll: But still—I know I'm also responsible, and whatever you do, like, I'm here to help. And to do that thing—

Jen: Support me.

Daryll: Right.

Jen: Thank you. That is—Thank you.

Pause.

Daryll: Jen—

Jen: What?

Daryll: Will you marry me?

Jen: No!

Daryll: Why not?

Jen: We're sixteen.

Daryll: So. We could live above the garage at my folks. I could go full time at the Burger Hut.

Jen: And quit school.

Daryll: Well—

Jen: Well what?

Daryll: I'm just trying to do the right thing.

Jen: So am I.

Pause.

Daryll: Did you tell your folks?

Jen: No.

Daryll: Cause if you tell your folks, they're gonna tell my folks.

Jen: I'll tell them if I want.

Daryll: Your Dad is gonna kill me.

Jen: You think he's not gonna kill me?

Daryll: How can you be pregnant?

Jen: THIS IS NOT MY FAULT, YOU KNOW?

Daryll: IT'S NOT MY FAULT EITHER!

Jen: SO WHAT DO YOU WANT FROM ME?

Daryll: I WANT YOU TO STOP YELLING BECAUSE IT'S NOT GONNA MAKE YOU ANY LESS PREGNANT!!!

Pause.

Daryll: Okay?

Jen: Okay . . .

Pause.

Jen: I just gotta weigh my options.

Daryll: Okay.

Jen: But I need your support.

Daryll: Totally. You got it.

Jen: I'll want to talk about it, and also about my feelings, and I know that's made you uncomfortable in the past.

Daryll: I'll be okay. Whatever you need.

Jen: Okay.

Pause.

Daryll: How can I support you, like, right now?

Jen: I don't know.

Daryll: You want some ice cream?

Jen: I would love some ice cream.

Daryll: You want some pickles?

Jen: No. I don't want any pickles.

Daryll: Okay . . .

They have a little laugh. Daryll starts the car.

Sign: LEO AND JOEY FIGURE IT OUT: PART TWO

Leo: You found out some more stuff?

Joey: Yeah. I went by a construction site. I feel a little dumb. I was way off last time.

Leo: So what did you find out?

Joey: It goes like this. You get a—you know.

Leo: I don't know anything.

Joey: You get a stiffy.

Leo: That much I know.

Joey: The girl: her thing is like a big flower. Like a rose, sort of.

Leo: Like a rose?

Joey: Right. So you gotta be careful of thorns.

Leo: I guess so.

Joey: But thorns or not, apparently it hurts like hell.

Leo: It hurts?

Joey: Oh yeah. You moan and groan like you've got the flu. It's gross.

Leo: But people do it?

Joey: You gotta do it, or they won't let you get a kid from the hospital.

Leo: Wow.

Joey: Yeah.

Leo: It's a weird world, Joey.

Joey: You can say that again.

Sign: BRAD AND BECKY HANG OUT

Becky has a camera and is setting up to take Brad's picture.

Becky: Okay. Sit here. More sideways. *She messes up his hair a little.* And the hair. And—I don't know. Read this. *Hands him a paper.*

Brad: Ah, the big city paper.

Becky: It costs extra, but it's worth it. I'm not gonna live here forever.

Brad: Head start.

Becky: That's the idea.

Brad: I like to read the personal ads.

Becky: Oh do you, now?

Brad: Yeah. It's like shopping for used humans.

Becky: *Snapping some pictures.* Anybody look promising?

Brad: Single white male, fifty-three, seeks woman, eighteen to twenty-eight, for friendship and frolicking. Must like stamps, my mother and have own teeth.

Becky: It doesn't say that.

Brad: No. I made it up.

Becky: What's your personal ad?

Brad: Uh . . . Single male, age unimportant, race unimportant, seeks soul mate for movie watching, trips to Cancun, and hockey games.

Becky: Hockey games? Why hockey games?

Brad: Cause I like hockey. That's why I've played since I was a kid.

Becky: I see.

Brad: You have a value judgement you'd like to express about that?

Becky: Well, it's none of my business, but I think hockey is stupid, and perpetuates violence and makes idiots rich while artists and scientists toil in obscurity for the betterment of humanity. Other than that, I think it's swell.

Brad: I see you have a strong prejudice.

Becky: No, I just have strong feelings.

Brad: May I rebut?

Becky: You can try.

Brad: There is violence in hockey, I agree. But there is also violence in film. Should there be no movies because we're afraid we'd see violence?

Becky: No, but that's—

Brad: No, that would be censorship. Are you for censorship?

Becky: No.

Brad: Also, I'll concede that professional hockey players are not known for their knowledge of literature and theoretical geometry . . . *Becky takes a picture* but they memorize a thousand plays, and learn hundreds of skating maneuvers. They are not idiots.

Becky: Some of them are.

Brad: And some of them aren't. I play hockey, and I flatter myself that I am not an idiot.

Becky: Well, you weren't a few minutes ago. *Becky takes a picture.*

Brad: And true, hockey players are rich. But there is money in hockey. So who should get it? The players who play, or the owners who . . . own.

Becky: *Sigh.* The players who play . . .

Brad: Plus, and this is the part you can't quantify . . . there is nothing like a solid cross-check. It's just—when the guy just flies off his skates and lands in a heap, it's the best ever.

Becky: Fine, Mr. Smarty-macho-pants. *Takes a picture.* Hockey's allowed.

Brad: Thank you very much.

Becky: I can't believe I took all these pictures of you liking hockey.

Brad: I like other stuff too.

Becky: That's why you're still here. *Beck moves very close to him. Look up. Takes his picture. Lowers her camera.* You know, a girl could get used to a mug like yours.

Brad: If a girl dated.

Becky: Yeah, you know, if—

Brad: Even if you did, Beck, it wouldn't work out.

Becky: I didn't say anything.

Brad: I'm just saying—

Becky: Shut up for a second. I'm taking a picture of your mouth.

Sign: JOEY AND LEO FIGURE IT OUT: PART THREE

Leo: Did you find out some more stuff?

Joey: Leo, our search is over. I got us a prime source.

Leo: Really? What? What?

Joey: *Down and Dirty* magazine. I found it under my brother's bed.

Leo: I dunno if we should be looking at that.

Joey: Leo, if our parents didn't want us to find out on our own they would've told us some stuff. I asked my Dad and all he did was unroll some kinda kitchen glove on a broomstick. We're on our own, Leo.

Leo: I guess you're right. Let's take a look.

Joey: *Reading.* I am twenty-two years old and a very successful lawyer. My friends tell me I'm very attractive and I'm also endowed with a . . .

They look closer.

Leo: That's less than two feet.

Joey: No it's not.

Leo: How do you figure?

Joey: Cause of the metric system.

Leo: Oh, right.

Joey: *Reading.* So when I went on my annual Hawaiian vacation, I took along my suntan oil and my sense of adventure. I arrived at a secluded beach and found I was not alone. I had surprised a tall attractive Hawaiian girl who had been skinny-dipping in the ocean.

Leo: Oh man.

Joey: She plopped down on my towel in front of me and said, "I need someone to rub lotion all over me. Can you help?"

Leo: Lemme see!

They put their heads together and read silently.

Signs: —WHAT THEY ARE READING
    —NEVER HAPPENED
    —WHAT THEY ARE READING
    —WAS WRITTEN BY A LADY LIKE THIS

An Edith Prickly type, with cat eye glasses, laughs and says.

Edith: Chew on that, you horny little buggers! HA HA HA HA HA HA HA HA HAHA HA HAHA HA HAHA HA HAHA HA HA HA!!!!

Leo: Wow.

Joey: Yeah.

Leo: Is all that true?

Joey: It's in a magazine, Leo. They couldn't publish it if it wasn't true.

Leo: Really?

Joey: They'd go to jail.

Leo: I guess.

Joey: Let's review what we've learned.

Leo: Okay. You have to be a lawyer.

Joey: Right.

Leo: You have to go to Hawaii.

Joey: Right.

Leo: You have to endowed with a—

Joey: Right.

Leo: And it happens regularly with complete strangers.

Joey: Right. And that's how sex works.

Leo: Simple enough.

Joey: I guess we don't need our parents to tell us stuff.

Leo: Not with this comprehensive guide.

Joey: Everything we need to know. I wonder where my brother got it.

Leo: Your parents probably gave it to him.

Joey: Yeah. They probably did.

Leo: You think it's worth it? I mean, law school, a trip to Hawaii, just to have sex?

Joey: I'm not sure.

Leo: Don't think I'm a wimp, but it's all kinda intimidating.

Joey: Kinda scary.

Leo: Yeah. Yeah.

Sign: BECKY SHARES A POEM.

Becky: Okay, you have to promise not to laugh.

Brad: I'm not gonna laugh.

Becky: I wrote this a long time ago. It's totally lame.

Brad: Don't say that. Just read it.

Becky: Okay—um—okay.

Brad: I'm listening.

Becky: Okay.

> I'm not very big, but I'm too big for here—
> This town, like a locked phone booth,
> Like a shoebox in a closet,
> Walls on all sides of me.
> No one can hear me screaming.
> No one can see me dreaming,
> Or knows me at all.

> That's it.

Brad: Wow.

Becky: It's terrible. I wrote it in grade eight.

Brad: It's not terrible at all. It's beautiful.

Becky: You think so?

Brad: Beautiful.

Becky: Say that again.

Brad: Beautiful?

Becky kisses him suddenly. Brad is uncomfortable. He pushes Becky back after a moment. Gently, but firmly. Becky is embarrassed and flustered.

Becky: I'm sorry.

Brad: It's okay.

Becky: Here I am, all no dating, and then I just throw myself at you. I feel like an idiot.

Brad: It's okay.

Becky: You just don't like me that way, right, you're just worried about our friendship and that it would be ruined if we dated right?

Brad: That's not it.

Becky: Then it's me. You are just not attracted to me in any way.

Brad: That's sort of it.

Becky: *In a flood.* Oh God. I'm a gigantic idiot. Just beat me to death right here, okay? I should've known better.

Brad: It's not you, Becky. It's me.

Becky: Oh sure, they always say that, it's not you it's me. I know, I've said it myself, and even the second I was saying it I was thinking, it's you pal. This all about you and how lame you are, so just spare me. Please-okay-thanks.

Brad: Becky this time it's not you. It's totally and completely me.

Becky: Really?

Brad: Honestly.

Becky: How so?

Brad: I'm gay.

Pause. Becky starts laughing.

Becky: I appreciate you sparing my feelings Brad—but— oh. Oh.

Pause.

Becky: Really?

Brad: Yes.

Becky: Oh.

Brad: That's kind of a secret, okay?

Becky: Of course.

Brad: Not that I'm a coward. It's just safer to wait until I get to a bigger town. To—ah—

Becky: Come out?

Brad: Yeah. That's what we call it.

Becky: It's catchy.

Brad: Thanks. So that's why I don't date. Not around here anyway.

Becky: Wow.

Brad: Yeah.

Becky: It's just so—but you can trust me, I swear.

Brad: I know.

Pause.

Becky: So . . . you're really gay?

Brad: Really and for true.

Twilla MacLeod as Becky and Collin Doyle as Brad.
PHOTO BY MIKE REICHERT STEINHAUER.

Becky: How do you know?

Brad: If you are, you know. There's no getting around it.

Becky: You think you might change your mind sometime?

Brad: I guess anything's possible. But—

Becky: But I shouldn't hold my breath?

Brad: You might turn blue.

Becky: Right . . .

Pause.

Becky: I wanna tell you a secret too.

Brad: You don't have to.

Becky: I know. But I gotta tell somebody, and this is the most intense sharing time I've had since the drama trip to Vancouver.

Brad: Okay.

Becky: The reason I don't date . . .

Brad: Yeah?

Becky: . . . is that, I just don't want to have sex, until I'm older. And probably until I live somewhere else. Cause sex can get you caught in a town like this. Like my cousin Laverne, and maybe—so, anyway, I'm, what-do-you-call-it . . . abstaining. And guys always want to, so I'm done with it. All of it. For now.

Brad: Wow.

Becky: You think I'm a dork?

Brad: No. It's cool. It's rebellious.

Becky: Rebellious?

Brad: Yeah. Everybody's having sex these days, but you're not. You're a rebel.

Becky: Yeah. Huh. I'm a rebel. Thanks Brad.

Sign: JEN VISITS LAVERNE

Jen: *Entering untidy apartment.* Hello? Hello?

Ben: MOM! MOM! Lady! LADY!

Laverne: Stop screaming Ben.

Overlapping.

    Ben: LADY! LADY! LADY!

        Laverne: Ben! Ben! Shhh! SHHHH! BEN!

Ben is quiet.

Laverne: Who are you?

Jen: Hello. I'm Jennifer Bennet. I called you yesterday morning?

Laverne: Right. I forgot. You're Becky's friend.

Jen: Yeah. And you're Becky's cousin.

Laverne: Right. And this is a school project or something?

Jen: Right. I'm doing this project on single mothers, and I—well, it's an essay, sort of, a project, I'm doing a diarama, as well, kind of a—why are you looking at me like that?

Laverne: You're lying to me.

Jen: I'm sorry?

Laverne: You oughta be. I'm a busy woman.

Jen: I didn't mean anything. I just—

Laverne: You're pregnant, aren't you?

Jen: Um—

Laverne: You're pregnant. And you want to see what you're in for.

Jen: Oh, that's not—

Laverne: Save it sweety. One of the up sides of being a fallen women is a keen perception of situations and a low low tolerance for crap. How far along are you?

Jen: Um—six weeks.

Laverne: It's early yet. You have all your options still.

Jen: What do you mean?

Laverne: You wait too long and you lose one of them . . . Abortion.

Jen: Oh. Yeah.

Laverne: So what can I do for you?

Jen: I just wanted to know what your life is like, mostly.

Laverne: Well it wasn't always as fabulous as this. I used to live in my Mom's basement.

Jen: Really?

Laverne: Sure. But then that lousy bum of a father starting paying support and I got a better part time job and now I can afford this lovely low income housing.

Jen: Were you in high school when—

Laverne: When Ben came along. Yeah. Grade eleven. When Ben was two, I finished through correspondence. It's harder than going to school.

Jen: Did you want to get married?

Laverne: To the father? No. For one thing, we were sixteen.

Jen: And now you're—

Laverne: Nineteen. I know, I hardly look it. I don't get a lot of sleep.

Jen: Do you regret anything?

Laverne: Keeping Ben? You bite your tongue, sister. I love my boy. I wouldn't trade him for anything.

Jen: I didn't mean—I probably seem really naïve.

Laverne: You want to know how hard it is to raise a kid on your own? Take how hard you think it is and multiply it by a million. I am so poor, I can't begin to tell you. I used to laugh at my Mom clipping coupons. Forty minutes of hunting to save thirty cents? Now I'm the queen of coupons. I used to think only losers lived in crappy places like this. Now I'm thrilled to live here. It's a step up for me. I used to think I needed eight hours of sleep. Now on a bad day, I can get by on forty minutes. Because I'm different than I was. And that's hard. But people do it. And maybe you can do it too. Oh geez, is that the time?

Jen: Yeah.

Laverne: I gotta get down to the laundry room before somebody steals my sheets. Single mothers always gotta go somewhere. Or they never get to go anywhere. Either way, there's always something to do.

Jen: Thanks for seeing me.

Laverne: You got somebody to talk to?

Jen: Oh, um—

Laverne: Because if you don't, I suppose you could come by once and while and talk to me.

Jen: Thanks.

Laverne: You got a coupla minutes to spare? Like, right now?

Jen: Yeah.

Laverne: Can you watch Ben for a minute while I get my sheets?

Jen: Sure.

Laverne: Thanks. Be right back Ben. You be good, alright?

Ben: Good. Goody Good!

Laverne: Be right back. *Exits.*

Jen: You're kinda cute, aren't you?

Ben: Cutie! Cutie pie!

Jen: You got a single Mom, huh?

Ben: Lady lady.

Jen: How's that working out for you?

Ben: Laddy blah.

Jen: How would that work out for me?

Jen and Ben look at each other for a moment.

Sign: JEN VISITS FATHER MICHAEL

Father: Hello. It's Jen, isn't it?

Jen: Yes, father. Jen . . . uh Smith.

Father: So, Jen Smith. What can I do for you?

Jen: Well father, I was just looking for some advice. You see, um, I'm in trouble.

Father: In what sort of trouble?

Jen: In trouble, in trouble.

Father: I don't follow.

Jen: I'm pregnant, Father.

Father: Oh, in trouble.

Jen: Yes.

Father: Nobody calls it that any more, I was confused.

Jen: Well—there it is.

Father: Yes. *Small pause.* Are you Catholic, Jen?

Jen: Well, my family is. I've been raised Catholic.

Father: But you're not so sure.

Jen: I just don't know if I can be a—good Catholic—about this.

Father: Confession can be a comfort at a time like this. God forgives.

Jen: Yes, and I'll confess, for sure, but right now I just need some advice.

Father: On what to do with your baby?

Jen: Yes.

Father: What do you want to do?

Jen: I want to do the right thing.

Father: You must know what I'm going to say.

Jen: I guess.

Father: That's a baby inside of you. A spark of divine life. That's not for you to destroy.

Jen: It's only a bunch of cells right now—

Father: That's not how we see it. What about adoption? So many people want a baby and can't have one. Wouldn't you like to provide that sort of love to a good home?

Jen: That sounds really nice and all, but—

Father: But what?

Jen: It doesn't seem that simple to me.

Father: I don't mean to suggest it's simple. I know nothing about this is simple. Except for God's law. And God's law says you must give your child life, if you can. To do otherwise would be a mortal sin.

Jen: I see.

Father: Would you like to confess? For the sake of comfort.

Jen: It couldn't hurt.

Father: Might help.

Jen: Okay.

Father: Okay. You have to start.

Jen: Okay.

Sign: JEN AND DARYLL ARE BACK FROM PLANNED PARENTHOOD

A scene in two settings: Becky's room and Daryll's room.

Becky: Hey, you're back.

Jen: Yeah.

Becky: How did it go?

Brad: Hey Daryll.

Daryll: Hey. Anybody miss me?

Brad: No. Everybody's out to dinner.

Daryll: Thanks for covering for me.

Brad: Least I can do.

Becky: So, "Planned Parenthood"?

Jen: That's what they call it.

Becky: Why not "Unplanned Parenthood"?

Jen: I think they're trying to be positive.

Brad: Are you okay?

Daryll: It's weird, man. I feel so helpless. All I do is take her places—

Becky: Daryll take you?

Jen: Yeah.

Daryll: And get her ice cream. I don't even think she likes the ice cream, anymore.

Jen: I didn't have to go all the way to *(nearest larger town or city)*. I could've just called.

Brad: So how'd it go at—uh—

Daryll: "Planned Parenthood."

Becky: Right.

Brad: Right.

Daryll: They're really nice.

Jen: It was nice to talk to somebody.

Daryll: They know all about everything.

Jen: I got all this information.

Daryll: But they made me wait outside, at first, you know—

Jen: But they didn't tell me what to do.

Daryll: Just in case I'm a tremendous jerk, this abusive man holding a gun on her or something.

Becky: So how does it work?

Jen: They have this counselling for all the options and all these pamphlets and if you want an abortion, they can set you up.

Becky: Pamphlets, eh?

Jen: They got pamphlets for everything.

Brad: You're not a jerk, Daryll.

Daryll: But some guys are.

Brad: That's why they keep you outside. At first.

Daryll: Right. Right. Makes sense.

Becky: What about these other pregnancy counselling places?

Jen: A lot of them aren't pro-choice. So if you want your choice—

Daryll: I'm just frustrated.

Becky: Right.

Daryll: And scared.

Brad: Yeah.

Daryll: I mean, am I gonna be a father to a kid I'm supporting? Am I gonna be father to a kid I'll never see? Or am I just gonna not be a father?

Jen: I asked them about abortion. I heard a lot about the other stuff already.

Daryll: I just wish there was a single idea I could start getting used to.

Brad: Jen's cool, Daryll. She'll make a good choice.

Daryll: Yeah.

Becky: So what's the deal?

Jen: It's covered by Health Care, at least for the moment. You have to go to the city. It takes ten minutes, but you have to be there for three hours.

Daryll: Yeah.

Jen: They recommend all this counselling before and after. Because a lot of people get depressed after. Hormones and guilt and that. Look, there's a pamphlet about it.

Brad: It sounds like she's really doing her research.

Becky: This is a lot of pamphlets.

Daryll: She's doing great. She's great. But—I'm still messed up.

Jen: I took one of each. You never know.

Brad: Of course, man.

Becky: So now you're done your research?

Jen: Pretty much.

Becky: So, what are you gonna do?

Jen: I don't know. I'm as messed up as ever.

Becky: Hang in there, girl.

Jen: Hanging in.

Daryll: Anyway. What have you been doing, man?

Brad: You know. Hanging around.

Jen: What's this picture?

Daryll: With who?

Jen: This is a picture of Brad.

Brad: You know. With Becky.

Jen: This is really a close up.

Becky: So?

Daryll: With Becky? I see.

Jen: You must have been right up against him to get a shot like this.

Brad: You see nothing.

Becky: Well you know. Anything for my art.

Daryll: I see nothing?

Jen: You like him?

Brad: Nothing to see here. Move along.

Becky: Sure I like him. I like milk. I like ice cream sandwiches too.

Daryll: Nothing to see here?

Brad: Nothing to see.

Jen: So you don't like him?

Daryll: So you don't like her?

Brad and Becky: Yeah I like him/her.

Brad: But—

Becky: It's not gonna work.

Brad: It's just not my bag.

Becky: We're friends.

Brad: We're good friends.

Becky: And that's that.

Jen and Daryll: Okay . . .

Sign: LEO AND JOEY SHARE THE WEALTH

Leo: I would like to thank you all for attending our seminar.

Joey: We have information to share that is vital to all of our futures.

Leo: The first part of our seminar in entitled "Sex and its relationship to Hawaii and the legal profession." We will begin with an instructional anecdote. Joey?

Joey: Thank you Leo. *Reading.* I am twenty-two years old and a very successful lawyer . . .

Jen enters.

Jen: Hey Leo, where's Becky?

Leo: She's in her room.

Jen: So, uh, what's going on? What are all these kids doing here?

Leo: We're conducting a seminar.

Joey: You can join us, if you want. It's a seminar about sex. This is our primary text. *Hands Jen the magazine.*

Jen: This is how you're learning about sex? And you two are teaching all these kids?

Leo: We're the most informed.

Jen: You're the most informed?

Joey: We're the ones with the magazine.

Jen: This magazine? Magazines are nothing Joey. I have pamphlets. *Pushes Leo and Joey aside.* Okay kids. I'm your new instructor. Listen up, cause I'm only gonna say this once. Sex can occur between any two consenting people, and it's better for everybody if those people are adults or somewhere close to it. It's best to start with foreplay, and that means to stimulate each other's genitals digitally or orally.

Joey: Digitally?

Leo: With a computer.

Joey: Yeah.

Jen: No. Digitally, like with these digits here on your hand, okay? Digits like fingers, alright? And then you guys'll get a stiffy—

Voices: We know—

Leo: But what is the girl's thing like?

Jen: Well . . . *Flips through the magazine* like this.

Leo: I knew it!

Jen: And then the stiffy is inserted into the vagina, like so.

Then you move it back and forth and that creates a pleasant friction and then before you know it, the man reaches orgasm. And that is basically sex.

Joey: That's sex?

Leo: Okay. Wow.

Joey: Thanks Jen. I think we all learned a lot.

Jen: I am so not even close to finished. When the man reaches orgasm, semen will be released from his penis and that semen contains hundreds of millions of sperm and each one of those sperm swims for all it's worth to try to find the egg. The egg is inside the woman and if just one, just one tiny little sperm makes it, that woman is pregnant and then you have to work at the Burger Hut for the rest of your life. And there's ways to stop it, sure, there's condoms if you have the guts to buy them, some places give them away but they're only in big cities and there's the pill if you can find a doctor that'll give it to you without telling your Mom and in a town this size, good luck.

Leo: Well, thank you Jen.

Joey: Yeah—

Jen: But there's more. There's diseases you can get. You can get a cytomegalovirus infection. It's part of the herpes family. The symptoms are sore throat, swollen glands, headache, fatigue and jaundice. There's Clymidia, it's more common than the flu, so watch out for a whitish, yellowish discharge and redness at the tip of your penis. And just when you thought it was safe to go back in the water, guess what's back? Syphilis! It's not just for Europe any-more! It starts with painless sores and swollen lymph nodes, but before you know it, arthritis, heart disease, blindness, paralysis and madness!

Leo: Thanks a lot Jen—

Jen: I'm just getting warmed up. What's behind door number three? Oops! Gonorrhea! Seems it's a bacterial infection that can lead to pelvic inflammatory disease, which can lead to sterility. And oh—what's that Mr. Hand?—Genital warts? Painless flesh colored growths on the penis or vulva? Can lead to cervical cancer in women? That sounds pretty nasty, Mr. Hand. But not as nasty as AIDS. That one's fatal. And you don't have to be gay to get that. That's a lie people tell to feel better. You might get off easy with just genital herpes. Just a bit of numbness and tingling and burning and watery blisters. It won't kill you, but it's incurable and contagious! But what am I talking about symptoms for? Most of these things don't even have symptoms. If you have symptoms, you're one of the lucky ones!

Joey: Thanks Jen—

Jen: Shut the hell up, Joey. I still have my conclusion. Sex is good. That message is everywhere you look. I don't have to tell you that. But there's another side to things, that everybody finds too icky to talk about. Now, I'm feeling a bit verbal lately, because I'm under a lot of stress, so let me say just this. Wait until you're older and then, don't be stupid.

Leo: Is that it?

Jen: Yes. No. These magazines. They are not the truth. This guy's a twenty-two-year-old lawyer? There's no such thing as a twenty-two-year-old lawyer. Lies! Lie lies lies! Thank you. That is all.

She storms out. Leo and Joey start clapping politely.

Sign: BRAD GOES HOME

Brad: Well, here comes the bus. I guess I gotta go.

Becky: Okay. You got my address.

Brad: I'll e-mail you.

Becky: I'll e-mail you back.

Brad: God bless the internet.

Becky: I'll miss you.

Brad: You won't have to. I'll visit.

Becky: Yeah, but—

Brad: I'll miss you too.

Becky: Can I try something here?

Brad: Sure, what—

Becky kisses him long and full on the mouth.

Brad: Huh.

Becky: Did that do anything for you at all?

Brad: Sorry.

Becky: It was worth a shot.

Brad: I can't be cured. This is me. Take it or leave it.

Becky: I'll take it.

Brad: You're the coolest Becky. You're gonna make some guy really happy.

Becky: You too.

Brad: Take care of yourself.

Becky: I will.

Brad: You promise?

Becky: Pinky swear.

Brad: Pinky sworn. Bye. *Exits.*

Becky: Just my luck.

SIGN: JEN DECIDES

Becky is reading. Jen comes into her room.

Becky: Hey.

Jen: Hey.

Becky: How are you doing?

Jen: Better. I just talked to Daryll. I decided.

Becky: Really? What are you going to do?

Jen: I'm gonna keep it.

Becky: Wow.

A bell sounds. The situation backs up.

Becky: Hey.

Jen: Hey.

Becky: How are you doing?

Jen: Better. I just talked to Daryll. I decided.

Becky: Really? What are you going to do?

Jen: I'm gonna put it up for adoption.

Becky: Wow.

A bell sounds. The situation backs up.

Becky: Hey.

Jen: Hey.

Becky: How are you doing?

Jen: Better. I just talked to Daryll. I decided.

Becky: Really? What are you going to do?

Jen: I'm getting an abortion.

Becky: Wow.

A bell sounds. The situation backs up.

Becky: Hey.

Jen: Hey.

Becky: How are you doing?

Jen: Better. I decided.

The End.

The winner of the Enbridge Award for Emerging Artist and three Sterling Awards for his work in Edmonton Theatre, Chris Craddock is one of Canada's finest young playwrights. Since graduating with a Bachelor of Fine Arts (Acting) from the University of Alberta in 1996, Chris has gone on to act in and direct his own plays, which have been performed all over Western Canada. Chris is currently involved in a number of theatrical endeavours and writing projects, including his adaptation of *Summer of My Amazing Luck* by Miriam Toews for Theatre Network.

Born in Kitchener, Ontario, Chris currently resides in Edmonton, Alberta where he eats greasy breakfasts and collects Incredible Hulk action figures.